Praise for
KINGDOM BUILDERS

Andrew has finally put into a book his heart and his passion for the local church and its financial well-being. I have known Andrew for 15 years and in that time, I have seen his heart and passion as a family man, an astute businessman, a generous kingdom giver, and an inspirer of men. His passion for financing the Kingdom is contagious and he has added value to churches around the world with his example, teaching, and personal revelation. It's one thing to write about what you know; it's quite another when you write because of who you are and what you are doing. I can certainly recommend this book to every member and pastor across the world as a resource for building faith and creating the right thinking for releasing resources for Kingdom building.

— **André & Wilma Olivier,** Senior Pastors,
Rivers Church South Africa

I have had the pleasure of knowing Andrew and his family for 20 years and have always had a high admiration of how their whole family has such a big heart for advancing the Kingdom of God, including the area of finances. As local pastors, we have seen Andrew minister in different settings. Whether it was a key note or one-on-one coaching, Andrew has been a vital part over the years of building our church. I am excited about getting this book into the hands of as many people as possible, as I know it will help people succeed in all areas of life, which is always Andrew's heart.

— **Thomas & Katherine Hansen,** Lead Pastors,
Hillsong Church Denmark & Malmö

He's the real deal. Andrew is tried and true. After knowing him for many years, I have seen and experienced his love for God, his love for his family, and his unswerving mission to finance and build God's Kingdom through the local church. Read, consider, and apply what's written here; you will be a bigger, better person.

— **Mark & Leigh Ramsey,** Senior Pastors,
Citipointe Church

I have known Andrew for many years and watched him on a personal level live the life he is passionate about teaching others. Where God, family, and career all flourish around the purpose he has found in building the local church. Every time he has been with us in Sweden, he has brought great revelation to our church about stewardship and how to build a life of purpose, whether it's been on the platform or through the many one-on-one conversations he has with people. This book will help you in many different ways.

— **Andreas & Lina Nielsen,** Lead Pastors,
Hillsong Church Sweden

Andrew had been a huge blessing to our church. As a long-time faithful member of Hillsong Church, he carries in him an insightful, inspiring, liberating perspective on what it means to partner with a pastor as a Kingdom Builder. I'm excited about this book!

— **Kevin & Sheila Gerald,** Senior Pastors,
Champions Centre Seattle

I have known Andrew Denton for many years and have watched his life unfold as a Kingdom Builder. He lives out the message in this book. His commitment to his family, his church, his business, and the Kingdom is a model for us all to live out so that our legacy lives on well beyond us.

— **Lee & Laura Domingue,**
Author of *Pearls of the King* and Founders of Kingdom Builders US

I have had the honor of knowing Andrew for many years. Along with his wife Susan, Andrew has lived with an unrelenting Kingdom passion, demonstrated in many ways, particularly their gift of giving. Andrew's book will inspire and equip you to live and build now for eternity.

— **Paul & Maree DeJong,** Senior Pastors,
LifeNZ New Zealand

It's been a real privilege to know Andrew Denton over many years and to have the chance to see the fruit of his life as a husband and father, as well as an Elder in our church. His faith for what God is able to do, his passion for the church, and his vulnerability in sharing from his life have all been an incredible blessing whether in person or in front of many. I know the authenticity of what's contained in these pages is going to genuinely impact people and result in incredible fruit in people's lives!

— **Chrishan & Danielle Jeyaratnam,** Campus Pastors,
Hillsong Church Perth

Andrew Denton is one of the finest men I know. There's something absolutely inspiring whenever I hear about his humble beginnings as a hard working plumber to the successful developer that he is today. Along with his wife Susan, Andrew's journey is one that speaks of grit, determination, faithfulness, and sacrificial generosity. The backside to Andrew's story is his obedience to God and is the substance that sends him around the world to equip and encourage people to discover and fulfill their God-given potential. Our people and church are better for his investment and have been challenged to be faithful with little, entrusted with much, and to push forward to build the Kingdom.

— **Mike & Lisa Kai,** Senior Pastors,
Inspire Church Hawaii

Andrew is one of my best mates. We met around 15 years ago and hit off a great friendship from the outset. Hanging with "The Don" as we like to call him, you soon get to know that "what the The Don says The Don does". I have had the privilege of traveling with Andrew on a number of occasions when he has shared his amazing Kingdom Builders story and observed him during one-on-one meetings as he listens and gives time, insight, and encouragement. His heart for the Kingdom of God is incredible and he works tirelessly to help people find their potential and purpose as he has definitely found his. This book is a great tool for pastors and churches; it will inspire and impact many.

— **Paul & Lizzie Clout,** Founders,
Paul Clout Design Australia

It has been said that the world will ask you two questions. Firstly, who are you (Identity)? Secondly, what are you doing here (Purpose)? If you don't have an answer, the world will tell you. For many years, I felt like a second-rate Christian. Whilst I knew my identity in Jesus, I struggled to know my purpose within business. Andrew is a cherished friend and mentor who helped me realize my God-given calling in the greater body of Christ. This is a book for the next generation of Christian Business Leaders and Kingdom Builders. The young men and women with a dream to be used by God, for God, within the sphere of business. You will identify with the openness and struggles, be encouraged by the stories of triumph, inspired as your heart opens to possibility, and equipped to live your God-given calling within business. Read it and be forever changed !

— **Peter & Clare Low,** Founders, 100x

Andrew is a great friend and inspiration to me. He is a man of God with clear Kingdom purpose, whose life has had a significant impact on myself, our church, and in the Kingdom of God. His generous spirit is both inspiring and contagious, as is his commitment to raising a generation of Kingdom-minded people. I am sincerely grateful for Andrew's investment into the Kingdom Builders of our local church and I know this has started an important journey and has set our people and our church up for the future. I believe this book with inspire you, expand your vision, and build your life.

— **Jostein & Britt Krogedal,** Lead Pastors,
Hillsong Church Norway

Andrew has to be one of the most inspiring men that I have met. Everything in his life speaks about authenticity and helping other people dream to live to their full potential. When I look at success, it's not just about finance and status, but about the whole picture: God, Family, Friendships, Love, and Legacy. For me, this is Andrew Denton. His life and story are a journey of faith, freedom, and living a life bigger and beyond himself by utilizing what he has in his hand to be a blessing to others and the Kingdom of God!

— **Brenden & Jacqui Brown,** Campus Pastors,
Hillsong Church San Fransisco

An encounter with Andrew Denton will change your life as it has changed mine. Andrew brings so much truth, wisdom, and authority when it comes to real life in the marketplace. What a privilege to draw from someone that lives a big purposeful life out of a deep relationship with Jesus.

— **Berend & Esther te Voortwis,** CEO, crowdbutching.com

I'm thankful God has allowed me to get to know Andrew Denton. As businessmen, we are good at focusing on WHAT we do and HOW we do it, but often times, we forget WHY we do it. Andrew's message about conducting our lives and businesses through Kingdom principles, but even more importantly—for Kingdom purposes—has changed my perspective on my God and has given me a calling to be a businessman.

— **David & Maren Reme,** CEO, Reme Holdings AS Norway

KINGDOM BUILDERS

HOW TO LIVE AN **ALL IN** LIFE THAT TURNS VISION INTO REALITY

Andrew Denton

Foreword by Brian Houston

First printing 2020
Cataloguing – in – Publication data available

ISBN 978-1-922-41104-4 (international trade paperback)
ISBN 978-1-922-41105-1 (audio)
ISBN 978-1-922-41106-8 (ebook)

Cover & interior design: Felix Molonfalean
Cover photography: Tony Irving

***To Susan** — you are truly a gift from God and the original Kingdom Builder in my life. This book is only possible because of your love, faith, and belief in me. Thank you for saying "yes" to this big, ugly Aussie.*

***To my children** — you are blessed to be a blessing. I know you know this and my prayer for you is that you would always be the head; not the tail. Keep the faith, stay on this path, and know your Mum and I love you.*

***To the Kingdom Builders all over the world** — keep going. Keep serving. Keep loving. Keep giving. Keep leading. And, stay "unoffendable".*

"Father God, I pray today:
Your will be done.
You've promised to guide my path.
Help me to make wise choices.
But give me favor with man. Amen."

CONTENTS

———

BRIAN HOUSTON

Andrew Denton is the kind of man every pastor wants in his congregation.

He's bold. He's honest. He's trustworthy. He has spiritual authority. He's a good husband, father, and grandfather. And he tells everyone that he's not a pastor, but he cares for people and extends himself to others as much, if not more, than any pastor I know.

I still remember the day he sat across from me over coffee during Hillsong Conference and confessed that he was feeling the 'call' to go and raise up Kingdom Builders across the globe. He felt to share his story and allow his story to inspire others to do the same. There was no ambition in his tone. He wasn't trying to build himself a platform or earn himself a name. He simply wanted others to experience the blessing that he himself has experienced through obedience to Christ.

When I sit back to think about the other men, women, and families in our church who represent our Kingdom Builders, the word that comes to mind is FAITHFUL. People who, just like Andrew, recognize the faithfulness of God in their own lives and who faithfully outwork His call to love thy neighbor, care for the poor, and reach the ends of the earth with the good news of the Gospel of Jesus Christ.

The Kingdom Builders of our own church have made significant personal sacrifices in order that the vision and mission of our church can take leaps and bounds forward and I don't know where we would be without them. They stretch and extend themselves. They believe that their lives can play a significant part in building the very thing that God Himself says He is building—His Church. The fruit of the weekly salvations we see at Hillsong Church is their fruit also—borne from a heart to make Hillsong— their place of planting—a HOME for others.

I believe that every pastor needs a core group of men and women just like this. People who love the House of God. People who are committed to leaning into the vision of their planting, to trusting and supporting leadership, and to Godly stewardship of what they themselves have been given.

I cannot encourage you enough to lean into this message and these principles that Andrew shares. If you are a pastor, pray that God brings you Kingdom Builders to help take your vision forward and give God the glory. If you are a business owner, a stay-at-home parent, a young person just starting university or anywhere in between, I pray that God would speak to you personally about the role that you can play, where He wants to take you, and how He wants to use your life to serve the world around you.

The Body of Christ is full of innovative men and women making a difference who recognize that Kingdom Builders are church builders; they recognize their lives are about more than themselves; they are men and women who have a revelation of the PURPOSE and CAUSE for which they are living. I pray that you, too, catch this revelation...

"O love the Lord, all you His saints! For the Lord preserves the faithful..." (Psalm 31:23 NKJV)

May God bless you and your family.

— **Brian Houston**
Global Founder and Senior Pastor, Hillsong Church
Bestselling author of *Live, Love, Lead*

Brotherly advice by

———

PHILL DENTON

My earliest memories of my big brother, Andrew, came down to two things: he was always working and he had a beard.

I was 10 when he moved out of home, 27 when we went into business together, and 20 years on from that, I can't imagine being in business with anyone else. Or doing anything else with my life.

We've both been blessed over the years and sought to be a blessing to others.

This book is Andrew's story. Over the years, I've been right there with him, shoulder to shoulder, and I've witnessed how God blesses steps of faith.

My advice to anyone reading is simple: you can do something.

You can give. It doesn't matter how much. Just as long as it's a step of faith. Something that stretches you. If you're thinking about it, then you just have to give it a go. So, back yourself. Go for it.

Hopefully, this book will help you take the first step. Especially, if you're being stirred and moved. That jab you feel in the ribs is God saying, "Take the jump."

— Phill Denton
Board Member, Hillsong Church
Kingdom Builder

AN INVITATION TO AN
ALL ———————— IN LIFE

I want to begin with a disclaimer: I never finished school. I'm just an Aussie plumber in clean clothes. There's nothing special about me. Except the fact I've chosen to go "all-in" with God.

Which brings me to the goal of this little book: I believe I've been called to mobilize a tribe of people to go "all-in" with God, too.

People just like my wife, Susan, and I.

Believers who have chosen to be faithful with what we have so God can open up the floodgates of Heaven.

I am writing this book because I believe God is raising up an army of Kingdom Builders all over the world.

I use the term Kingdom Builder because we are not called to be Kingdom passengers.

We're not called to be Kingdom consumers.

No.

We are called to be Kingdom Builders.

I know a thing or two about building. I've been doing it all of my life.

Being a Kingdom Builder is not about intelligence, skills, or social standing.

It's not about your financial position.

Trust me, my wife and I didn't have much when we took our first step of faith. At the time, it seemed impossible. But, we trusted God and He has more than blessed us a thousand times over.

I genuinely believe we're blessed to be a blessing. I didn't always think this way. Now, it's my sole mission in life to share this simple, life-changing truth.

God is inviting you to help build His Kingdom.

Yes.

He's calling you to be a Kingdom Builder.

Being a Kingdom Builder is about faith.

Believing the promises of the Scriptures. Making wise choices. And, following God daily.

I want to stress daily. Faith is a moment-by-moment journey with God.

In the following pages, I share my story and the stories of others who have heard the call of God to finance the Kingdom. Ordinary people just like you who have woken up to the joy of what it means to live a generous life. Believers who have stepped over the line and decided to put God first in every area of their lives.

I hope you'll join us.

EXACTLY THE SAME FAITH

My great-grandfather was kicked out of the Baptist Church for being too spiritual. He was a simple tradie like me who was radically saved. Pop Denton was my first example of what it meant to be "all-in" as a believer. He used to preach on the street corners in Sydney about the one true God.

I am grateful to him for setting the Denton family on course for multiple generations of believers. His son, Sidney, my grandfather, was a pastor. My father, Barry, was as well. On my wife's side of the family, Christianity also goes back multiple generations. We have a rich Christian heritage.

My wife, Susan, and I have three children: Jonathan, who is married to Kmy and who gave us our first grandson, Dallas, and granddaughter, Daisy; Mitchell, who is married to Elisabetta; and, our daughter, Anna, who is married to Ehsan, with our granddaughter, Sage.

All of our children are in church and serving God.

I was born in 1965 in Bowral, New South Wales, Australia. I have been in church most Sundays for the past 55 years. Growing up, all I knew was church. Being a pastor's kid can either drive you straight into ministry or away from pastoring altogether. I chose to surf and work.

Don't get me wrong, I love pastors. I just don't want to be one.

I still feel the same way today. In fact, my opening line when I get up to share the message of Kingdom Builders is this:

"I'm not a pastor. I'm not on staff at Hillsong Church. I'm not an itinerate speaker. I don't do this for a living. Ninety-nine percent of the time, I sit in the congregation like you—because I am you!"

The only difference between the old Andrew and the new one is that today, I know who I am. I know my purpose in life: to finance the Kingdom.

I didn't always think this way. Being brought up as a Pentecostal preacher's kid (PK) in the sixties and seventies, we inherited a poverty mindset. Basically, the belief that if you were rich, you were dodgy; money was definitely the root of all evil. This teaching was all I knew.

My dad always had a side-hustle to compensate for his pastor's salary. I knew when it was the end of the month because we ate spaghetti the whole week for dinner.

Yet, something about the poverty mindset just didn't sit well with me, but I didn't know any other way to think about finances at the time.

At home, church came first and family came second.

Growing up, I never excelled in school. In fact, I loathed it and I would skip a lot of classes. The ocean was the place I felt the most peaceful, accepted, and challenged. I've been a surfer all my life. I surfed before school, after school, and during school. So, as soon as I could legally leave school, I did.

At the ripe old age of 15, I left my formalized education to enter the workforce with no real plan other than to get an apprenticeship in a trade.

I had no clue what I wanted to do so I went to the Careers Night at a Trades Show Expo. If I'm honest with you, I wanted to get the most for doing the least.

I went table by table that night, asking one simple question:

"How much do you pay?"

Plumbing paid the highest as an apprentice, so I chose to become a plumber.

No research. No forward thinking. Just who paid the most.

I sent off a handful of resumes to prospective employers and went to a couple of interviews before heading off on an extended surf trip with a good mate. About a week before I was due home, I rang my mother who hadn't heard from me in weeks. I told her I would be home the following Tuesday.

Her reply was pretty straightforward and shocking, "Good. You have a job and you start on Wednesday!"

So I began my professional life as a plumber's apprentice.

One thing my father taught me was to work hard. I'm grateful for this, but I didn't have a good grasp on finances. It wasn't until I was 16 and I met my then girlfriend, and future wife, Susan, that I began to get a better understanding of money.

I met her at church on a Sunday morning. Someone knew of my father's church and recommended she come along. I still remember what she was wearing the first time I saw her.

To say she impressed this big, ugly Aussie bloke would be an understatement. She had this unshakeable belief that God had so much more for her.

One of the first questions she ever asked me was, "What's your five-year plan?"

I responded, "What's a five-year plan?"

To which she said, "You know, your goals and dreams for the future?"

I sat there staring at her. I had never thought further than the coming weekend. I didn't know what to say.

The only thought that came to my head was, "I'd like a hot car!"

Susan was shocked. She couldn't believe I had never dreamed about owning my own business or my own home. All the things she had desired since she was 10!

Susan taught me about finances. She has always been a saver.

In fact, when I met her, she was on her first stop of a

world-tour she had planned by saving her pocket money from when she was a small child. She figured she needed to go on this big adventure and then buy her first home in New Zealand. And since buying a house would be a major expense and she knew she would be locked in, and not do anything but work, she decided to go on a working holiday to Australia first.

Now as a 19-year-old qualified hairdresser from New Zealand, she crossed paths with this big, Aussie bloke who could work hard, but had no plans for the future.

Two years later, we bought our first home together. Susan supplied most of the deposit and I co-signed because back then, you needed a man to get a mortgage. I was just 18 and a third-year apprentice at the time, but she could see the bigger picture of what God was doing.

I lived in that little red-brick house on Nattai Street with a bunch of mates for the next two years until we finally married. On our first wedding anniversary, we found out Susan was pregnant. Life suddenly became very hard.

I was gobsmacked when she told me the news. For the first time in my life, I realized I was responsible for somebody else.

Jonathan was born and we were down to one wage. Interest rates in Australia were at an all-time historical high in 1987, around 18%. I had the monumental task on my hands of providing for my family. I did what my father taught me to do: work hard.

Over the next 10 years, I hustled. I've never been afraid of work.

Six days a week? No problem.

Eighteen-hour days? Andrew's got it.

I don't regret those early days. I learned a lot about faithfulness and fulfilling my promises.

When I was 21 years old, we had a visiting prophet come to my father's church. I had known this guy since I was a young kid and had heard him preach many times before, so I wasn't expecting what was about to happen.

He spoke out over the congregation and proceeded to prophesy over me about the mantle for ministry that was on my father the pastor, on my grandfather the pastor, and even on my great-grandfather. He prophesied their mantle of ministry was the same mantle on me.

He also prophesied my ministry would be one not everyone could do.

To say I was shocked that day would be an understatement.

I mean, I certainly knew I didn't want to be a pastor. So, I disagreed with him about that detail. But, what was this other ministry?

Isn't the only ministry to be a pastor? What else could he mean? I was confused. I put it in the back of my mind completely forgetting about it.

The next phase of my life involved working full-time as a plumber for a boss, my own plumbing business also, and a multi-level marketing business, too.

Work, work, and more work.

It's all I did.

It breaks my heart to admit it, but we didn't have a

family holiday for eight years.

During that season of life, I became a very boring, tired, and depressed man. I was still going to church with my family. I was still singing the praise and worship songs. But, I was dead inside.

I will never forget the day I arrived home at 5 o'clock in the afternoon to quickly shower and eat some dinner, before heading back out to work, when Susan said to me, "You do know, I'm a single mother with three kids, don't you?"

In my ignorance and defense I said, "What a stupid statement. Of course you're not a single mother! You're married to me!"

She replied, "That doesn't change the fact I'm a single mother with three kids."

I shot straight back at her, "Well, I'm here aren't I?"

And she shot back, "You are never here, Andrew. All you ever do is work, work, work!"

I'm fired up at this point and past the point of anger said, "I'm doing it for the family."

"What family?" Susan said. "Andrew, something has to change!"

I stormed out of the house, slammed the front door, jumped in my truck, and drove off. I only got a few kilometers down the road before I had to pull over. I was weeping at what had just happened. Big, ugly tears.

I was angry and upset.

This wasn't where I wanted to be in life. Here, I was a true workaholic, in danger of losing my family.

I had no purpose. I had no true 'why' behind my daily choices. I realized I was only financially providing for my family and not very well at that. I was working so much; I had lost where I fitted into my family and how to be a present husband, father, and family man.

As I sat in my truck on the side of the road with tears bucketing down my cheeks, I knew I needed to get some help.

I turned my truck around and drove straight back home to Susan. I apologized for my actions and the way I was living. She suggested I go and speak to one of the pastors at church.

I knew she was right, but I hated what she was asking me to do. Up until that point in my life, I thought counseling was for weak people. So, I swallowed my pride and reached out for help.

Speaking to one of our pastors was absolute gold. He pointed me straight back to Jesus and said I needed to ask Him for direction in my life and for what specific changes I needed to make.

So, I diligently started to pray and seek God like I had never done before in my life.

A few weeks later, I attended a men's camp that my church, Hillsong Church, was putting on. It was there that my pastor, Brian Houston, preached a message on the "Faith of the Centurion" from Matthew 8:5-13.

I was sitting on the front row. Not because I was special. Because I was eager. Open and ready to learn.

At that time, we were the largest church in Australia,

14 years into our journey, with thousands of members, and we didn't have a building.

Now, let me tell you something about Hillsong Church. Pastor Brian and Bobbie Houston pioneered this church from a school hall in 1983 into the thriving global congregation it is today. But it was never about numbers.

They used whatever resources they had to build community. The wealth of our church—I will say this over and over again throughout this book—is the PEOPLE.

Buildings are not about the latest technology, about prestige or erecting monuments to ourselves—they are about housing the work of God and facilitating space for people to find community, fellowship, and ultimately, relationship with Jesus.

We were using whatever means we had to gather and grow—school halls and community centers—but we were consistently at the mercy of a landlord. Spending hours of precious volunteer time bumping in and out of venues, and not building for our future.

This frustrated a visionary like Pastor Brian to no end. Our church was filled with faithful, everyday, hard-working people—not wealthy millionaires. The solution looked impossible. It was in this season that God gave Pastor Brian a word that it wasn't about finding one or two wealthy individuals to carry the load; it was about raising up an entire generation of generous men and women who would carry the long-term vision, believing that God also wanted to bless them to be a blessing.

That was when God spoke to him a message about the

faith of the Centurion. And it was then that he spoke it over us at this men's camp. Right when I'm at a breaking point in my own life.

It's a famous story. Here's my paraphrased version: The Centurion comes to Jesus and asks Him to heal his servant. Jesus was like, "Sure, let's go to your house and heal your servant."

The Centurion replies, "Hold on, Jesus. First of all, I'm not worthy of you coming to my house. Secondly, you don't even need to come to my house. You just say the word and my servant will be healed."

And the Scriptures tell us that Jesus was amazed at this man's faith.

The Centurion's like, "Faith? This has nothing to do with faith. This has to do with authority. I'm a man of authority. And, I'm actually a man under authority. I say to this man, 'You go over there.' And, he goes over there. Aren't you the same, Jesus? You're a man of authority. So, just say the word and my servant will be healed."

Pastor Brian points out in his message that the Centurion had 100 men under his authority who would do whatever was required, not as robots, but as willing participants for the cause of Rome.

Pastor Brian then says, "Guys, this is amazing. As your Senior Pastor, I've worked out what I need. I need 100 men who will do whatever is required for the sake of the Kingdom, not as robots, but as willing participants for the Cause of Christ. The first thing I'm going to ask this group to do is raise $1,000,000 over and above normal tithes and offerings."

When I heard Pastor Brian say those words, it was like a bang, "This is me"—my heart leapt out of my chest!

I had no clue how I was going to raise the money. However, I walked straight up to Pastor Brian a blubbering mess and said, "I'm in."

I'm sure he looked at me and thought, "Wow, that's nice, Andrew. This will be interesting." Because at that point of my journey, my life was out of sorts.

I gathered a few guys around Pastor Brian that night. We prayed for him and that's how Kingdom Builders started.

It was 1996. That day was so pivotal in my testimony and in the testimony of Hillsong Church.

If you know anything about church and finance, normal weekly tithes and offerings are what keep the lights on and, hopefully, pay the pastor's salary. It's the 'over and above' offerings, which help the Church take giant leaps of faith, buy buildings, start satellite campuses, and spread the Gospel around the globe.

In 1997, the first Kingdom Builders offering came in.

The first year of Kingdom Builders, God told Susan and I to write a check for $5,000. It might as well have been $5,000,000. At the time, I was working two jobs and running another business from home. That year, I gave up the night job to be with my family.

And, you know what? We wrote that check.

Somehow with less, God blessed us with more.

It was a faith step for us as a family, but Susan and I

knew this is what God was calling us to do.

The first year we took this step of faith, we made massive changes in our lives. It was scary, but also massively exciting. It was the first year I didn't rely on Andrew. It was incredible. At the end of the year, we had this $5,000 to drop in the container.

So, I said to my wife, "Let's do it again."

I remember clearly also bringing the kids on the journey. I said to them, "Last year, we gave $5,000. This year, we're giving $15,000."

At the time, we were driving a $10,000 car. One of the things I'd done to put capacity in my life was to sell my nice car and buy a less expensive one. It was good for my ego and I also did it because I needed to live by a newfound conviction: opportunity comes to those who prepare themselves.

I put time in my life again. I put capacity in my life again when it came to finances. It was a big swallowing of my pride, but I was able to write a $15,000 check.

I remember very clearly thinking to myself in the church parking lot, "This is scary again. It's exactly the same faith to give $15,000 as it was last year to give $5,000."

It was amazing.

Only two years later, we wrote a check for $80,000.

Two years after that, we wrote a check for $240,000.

This was blowing me away.

Here I was for 10 years slaving my guts out, relying totally on Andrew, basically failing in every area of my life. Here we were, a few short years later, and the only thing we'd done differently was answer this question: "Do we trust God or not?"

We were either "all in" or "all out".

Here we were writing a $240,000 check just a few years later.

Why?

Because we had chosen to go "all-in" and believe the promises of God.

Up to the point where we wrote the $5,000 check, Susan and I had only been tithers. After we chose to step over the line and give sacrificially, God blew the lid off of our lives.

The $5,000 check was used towards the building of Hillsong's first building. Susan and I were there in the nosebleed section when it opened. On the night, a prophecy was given that in the future, Hillsong Church would see multiple million-dollar checks.

Aussies can get excited when they need to and there was a standing ovation. And it went for a long time. I know it went for a long time, because I had a whole conversation with my wife during the ovation.

I remember saying, "That's crazy."

Susan said to me, "Wouldn't it be awesome if ordinary people in our church were raised up and gave that, not just millionaires getting saved?"

I remember thinking to myself, "That is ridiculous. That's above what you can ask, think or imagine. That is really crazy stuff."

But the Holy Spirit spoke through Susan that night. I

don't think she knew. Certainly, I didn't have a clue that within eight years, my brother Phillip, his wife Melissa, Susan, and I together, would write that $1,000,000 check from our business.

Was it scary?

Absolutely.

Was it exciting?

Unbelievably so.

But no more scary or exciting than when we wrote the $5,000. Because it was exactly the same faith.

When my brother, Phill, and I had that $1,000,000 check, I remember saying, "Let's not just drop this in the offering container in case they lose this sucker. Let's make an appointment with Pastor Brian."

When we handed it to him, he looked me directly in the eyes and said, "You know, I'm not going to treat you any differently to anyone else."

I said, "Good. In fact, please don't tell anyone who gave this because at some point this weekend, some other couple is going to give $5,000 and it's going to take exactly the same faith."

And, every year, we keep taking steps of faith. The checks today have more zeroes, but it's the exact same faith as when we gave $5,000. The exact same faith.

Over the last six years, God has taken me all over the planet to raise up people who will go "all-in". Kingdom Builders who will finance the Cause of Christ. Men and women who will willingly sacrifice and give to advance the Kingdom.

Maybe you're like the way I used to be back in 1996. Lost. Tired. Searching for purpose.

I would venture to say, your purpose is to help your local church beyond what even your senior pastor can ask, think or imagine.

Susan and I have been blessed to be a blessing.

The same calling and opportunity are yours.

The following pages will hopefully help you find the courage to answer the call to finance the Kingdom.

I've divided the book into three parts: The Principles, The Partners, and The Practice.

The first section will help you understand biblically what it means to be a Kingdom Builder. The second section will help you understand and identify the team you'll need around you to be faithful. The final section is a practical guide to help you get started and to keep on going no matter what.

As I tell people all over the world who ask me if Kingdom Builders is exclusive:

I always reply, "Yes, it's exclusive. But everyone's invited."

Will you choose to be a Kingdom Builder?

I hope so. It's not easy. However, it's incredibly simple.

It just requires you to surrender.

Here's how...

PART ONE

———

THE PRINCIPLES

THE MINISTRY OF WHAT?

———

As I stated in the opening chapter, I'm not a pastor.

My ministry is not to shepherd people.

It's not to lead from the platform in praise and worship.

My ministry is to finance the Kingdom.

And, it's easy for me to trust my pastor and do my part. We've both been called into ministry.

In 29 years of being a part of Hillsong Church, I've never ever been to a church service where someone hasn't been saved. I've been all over the world in all kinds of services and I've seen the fruit.

So, now it's not hard to write a check.

It's not hard to sacrificially give.

It's not hard to challenge others to do the same.

God just asks me to be the giver. God asks me to provide it. Not to give with strings attached. Not to be picky about where the money is going. But to faithfully give and trust Him at His word.

God asks me to be a willing participant. I don't have a say. Neither do you.

When I talk about the ministry of financing the Kingdom, I'm talking about actively participating and giving to what's going to take the Church forward.

The above and beyond offering.

Not just the normal tithes and offering, which keep the lights on. Pays the pastor's salary. That's easy. It's the over and above giving that makes the biggest difference in the Kingdom.

I'm amazed at how many people don't trust God with their finances.

The sad truth is people just don't tithe. I've seen it over and over again across the world. People too afraid to give 10% back to God. Which is the least of what He's commanded us to do.

This lack of faith holds the Church back from taking giant leaps of faith like opening new campuses across the city, let alone across the world.

That's the "over and above" money. The sacrificial offering.

As a business man, I like to see impact. I don't have to look any further than my own children to see the impact of my giving. Anything we've ever given to the church—every dollar, every hour, every sacrifice—has been worth it. Simply for the impact our giving has had on our family.

Totally worth it.

THE CORE OF THE CORE

We have this Heart for the House offering at Hillsong Church. It's when the Kingdom Builders' giving culminates annually. After our 2014 offering, I went and spoke to the CFO of Hillsong Church in Australia because I wanted to know what impact Kingdom Builders was having as an overall percentage of the Heart for the House offering.

It took him three weeks to figure out the number; I guess because he had to check, check, and re-check the numbers. When he called me into his office, he had his two senior accountants in his office to back him up.

What he found blew me away.

The really amazing thing, and the greatest surprise, was that the largest percentage of that offering—70%—was given by a small, but faithful and generous group of people—the Kingdom Builders. People who had a revelation of what generosity can do in their lives and the lives of others, when they themselves become the conduit for that blessing to flow.

Now, you may be reading this and thinking to yourself, "I'm not a millionaire."

Well, neither was I when Susan and I wrote our first check. Which is why the minimum commitment of giving to be a Kingdom Builder is $5,000.

You see, being a Kingdom Builder is not about how much you give. It's about your heart. Sacrificially giving above and beyond your normal tithes and offering.

I get asked all the time, "Isn't Kingdom Builders exclusive?"

And I say, "Absolutely. It's just open to everybody."

It's a little bit like asking who gets to hold the microphone on platform during praise and worship on a Sunday. The creative team is open to everyone. You come along and serve. You prove yourself. And, you don't even have to be the best singer to lead worship. You just have to have the best heart.

Kingdom Builders is a heart condition.

It's a group of committed people who have decided to put God first in every area of their lives.

THE PARABLE OF THE TALENTS

Jesus tells a story in the Gospels about the kind of people He is looking for to build His Kingdom. When talking about the Kingdom of God, Jesus says:

> "It's also like a man going off on an extended trip. He called his servants together and delegated responsibilities. To one he gave five thousand dollars, to another two thousand, to a third one thousand, depending on their abilities. Then he left. Right off, the first servant went to work and doubled his master's investment. The second did the same. But the man with the single thousand dug a hole and carefully buried his master's money.
>
> "After a long absence, the master of those three

servants came back and settled up with them. The one given five thousand dollars showed him how he had doubled his investment. His master commended him: 'Good work! You did your job well. From now on be my partner.'

"The servant with the two thousand showed how he also had doubled his master's investment. His master commended him: 'Good work! You did your job well. From now on be my partner.'

"The servant given one thousand said, 'Master, I know you have high standards and hate careless ways, that you demand the best and make no allowances for error. I was afraid I might disappoint you, so I found a good hiding place and secured your money. Here it is, safe and sound down to the last cent.'

"The master was furious. 'That's a terrible way to live! It's criminal to live cautiously like that! If you knew I was after the best, why did you do less than the least? The least you could have done would have been to invest the sum with the bankers, where at least I would have gotten a little interest.

" 'Take the thousand and give it to the one who risked the most. And get rid of this "play-it-safe" who won't go out on a limb. Throw him out into utter darkness."

(Matthew 25:14-30)

There are a few key principles we can take away from this passage.

For starters, Jesus is looking for people who are willing to "go out on a limb" financially. Believers who aren't afraid to trust Him at His Word and take healthy risks for the Cause of Christ.

We can also see in this story that God is looking for partners. Willing participants. People searching for purpose just like I was back in 1996.

Too many Christians are spectators.

God is looking for active participants.

People He can trust. Regardless of ability or income.

The first two servants invested what they had been entrusted with, yet the third failed to believe the promises of God.

Don't gloss over this simple Kingdom principle: when you invest what God gives you, it grows. When you act on what He's commanded you to do, He blesses that step of faith.

Sadly, we also see what happens to those who live a life of fear like the third servant.

What you have is taken from you. Even worse than that, your lack of faith cuts you off from genuine community.

That's what's amazing about Kingdom Builders. It's the core of the core in church. There's a core in any church. Typically, 25-30% are actively serving and maybe tithing. But, it's the one percent who make the difference.

Kingdom Builders who are "all-in".

In Stockholm, Sweden, when I helped launch Kingdom Builders six years ago, they were about to lose their building. Five years later, they now have six campuses and own two properties.

Why?

The core of the core, the Kingdom Builders, stepped up.

Today, Kingdom Builders make up almost 10% of their total congregation. The church in Stockholm has become the poster child of the impact Kingdom Builders can have.

SO YOU WANT TO BE A KINGDOM BUILDER?

I've talked a lot about finances in this opening chapter, but let me be clear: being a Kingdom Builder is not about money.

The first requirement to be a Kingdom Builder is the decision to put God first in all areas of your life.

To "burn your boats". To shake off complacency. To step over the line. To go "all-in" with God. A no-looking-back leap of faith that isn't for the faint-hearted.

It's about trusting all the promises of God. And, believing every single one of God's promises is meant for you.

Is it easy?

No.

Is it worth it?

Absolutely!

The second requirement of being a Kingdom Builder is to believe in the vision of the church. No matter what church you're a member of, you have to fully support the future of your faith community.

The third requirement for being a Kingdom Builder is

to say in your heart, "Pastor, I've got your back." You have to support the leader of your faith community. You have to fight with him and for him.

I haven't always agreed with my pastor, but I've always had his back. And, he knows he can count on me.

In my personal experience, what I have seen in my life and the lives of other Kingdom Builders, is money flows as a consequence of the first three Kingdom Builder requirements. But, you have to get your heart right first.

I was once speaking at a Kingdom Builders event and a young man approached me at the end of my talk. I looked at this young guy and he's covered in tattoos from head to toe. I recognize him from One80TC, a drug and alcohol rehabilitation service; he's just come out of jail and enrolled in Bible College. He's turning his life around.

He walks up to me with a big smile on his face and I remember thinking he was going to say, "Yeah, thanks, Andrew. But I can't do this."

Instead, he says to me, "Andrew, I'm in. I've worked out that if I just give up coffee, I'm halfway there to $5,000."

I said to him, "Mate, that's the right answer. That's the right attitude. It's not why you can't do it, but it's why you can."

When you think about it, as an ex-addict, the only thing the guy probably had left was coffee! And truly, I don't think most people are prepared to give up coffee. But, he was so moved to give up this last stronghold, to say "yes" to something bigger than himself.

Here's a man who had been saved from much. He was

destined for jail. No one does well when they go to jail. They don't come out of there better, they come out of there worse. But, he was fortunate enough that the judge sentenced him to go to rehab. And, in rehab, he found Jesus.

Today, he's a married man, out of debt, a new home-owner, actively serving, and giving.

That's the type of heart God is looking for. That is the heart of a true Kingdom Builder.

ALL THINGS

The main passage God has used in this whole Kingdom Builder journey is in the Gospel of Matthew:

> "Therefore I tell you, do not worry about your life, what you will eat or drink, or about your body, what you will wear. Is not life more than food, and the body more than clothes? Look at the birds of the air; they do not sow or reap or store away in barns, and yet your heavenly Father feeds them. Are you not much more valuable than they? Can any one of you by worrying add a single hour to your life?
>
> "And why do you worry about clothes? See how the flowers of the field grow. They do not labor or spin. Yet I tell you that not even Solomon in all his splendour was dressed like one of these. If that is how God clothes the grass of the field, which is here today and tomorrow is thrown into the fire, will he

not much more clothe you—you of little faith? So do not worry, saying, 'What shall we eat?' or 'What shall we drink?' or 'What shall we wear?' For the pagans run after all these things, and your heavenly Father knows that you need them. But seek first his kingdom and his righteousness, and all these things will be given to you as well. Therefore do not worry about tomorrow, for tomorrow will worry about itself. Each day has enough trouble of its own.

(Matthew 6:25-34 NIV)

In verse 33, Jesus is basically saying, "Trust God—and all things will be given to you."

What are "all these things" in my life?

As a Kingdom Builder, I should have the best marriage.

As a Kingdom Builder, I should have the best relationship with my children.

As a Kingdom Builder, I should be fit and healthy.

Why do I mention these three things? Because they are a part of my "all".

What is your "all"?

In the verses leading up to verse 33, Jesus is talking about the things the world is chasing after. The world is focused on getting.

God is looking for people who know in their heart that this life is about giving.

There's a promise hidden here: when you put God first, all things will be given to you. But, you have to seek Him first. Not stuff. Not material possessions. Not wealth.

There's nothing wrong with nice stuff. I like the stuff. But, it's not what I'm seeking after.

God's taught me it's okay to have nice stuff, as long as the stuff doesn't have me.

And, that's the beauty of Kingdom Builders.

We know God has our back, and is for us. We can trust Him to be our All.

SEEING GOD AS MY ALL

The first 10 years of my career, I was chasing the big house, the nice cars, the big life.

And, I was doing that by putting me first.

Me providing...

Me working my tail off...

Me hustling...

Me. Me. Me. Me. Me.

Not by seeing God as my Source.

The big reveal to me was when I actually put God first—then everything really happened.

Over the years, I've seen God work in ways above and beyond anything I could ask, think or imagine. I used to think Ephesians 3:20 was the most ridiculous verse in the Bible:

> God can do anything, you know—far more than you could ever imagine or guess or request in your wildest dreams! He does it not by pushing us

around but by working within us, his Spirit deeply and gently within us.

Really? Beyond anything I could ask, think or imagine? Really, God?

Twenty-four years ago, I was on $100,000 dollars, which was a great salary back then. I was paid well. I worked for the largest plumbing company in Australia, running really big projects with 50 plumbers working underneath me. I was a good worker, but to think I could ever earn $1,000,000 in one year...

Well, that's just ridiculous.

But to give $1,000,000?

You've got to earn a whole lot more than a million to be able to give a million.

I'm telling you, over the years, I've seen God provide, and provide, and provide. Susan and I have continually seen Ephesians 3:20 in our lives.

You see, the world is looking for the one thing it can do to unlock blessing and fortune. Libraries and bookstores are full of these books.

And, I believe as Christians, we've got it.

When you put God first, everything flows as a consequence. Opportunity flows. Resources flow. The heavens literally are poured out.

Malachi 3:6-12 says:

"I am God—yes, I Am. I haven't changed. And because I haven't changed, you, the descendants of

Jacob, haven't been destroyed. You have a long history of ignoring my commands. You haven't done a thing I've told you. Return to me so I can return to you," says God-of-the-Angel-Armies.

"You ask, 'But how do we return?'

"Begin by being honest. Do honest people rob God? But you rob me day after day.

"You ask, 'How have we robbed you?'

"The tithe and the offering—that's how! And now you're under a curse—the whole lot of you— because you're robbing me. Bring your full tithe to the Temple treasury so there will be ample provisions in my Temple. Test me in this and see if I don't open up heaven itself to you and pour out blessings beyond your wildest dreams. For my part, I will defend you against marauders, protect your wheat fields and vegetable gardens against plunderers."

The Message of God-of-the-Angel-Armies.

"You'll be voted 'Happiest Nation.' You'll expe rience what it's like to be a country of grace."

God-of-the-Angel-Armies says so.

It's the one Scripture in the whole Bible where God asks us to test Him. And, Susan and I have. And you know what?

He's out given us every time.

Time and time again, God has poured down blessing upon us and our family.

REVELATION

For me, the next phase of my Kingdom Builder journey started when I got the calling to raise others up to finance the Kingdom. Pastor Brian asked me to become one of the Elders at church. It genuinely freaked me out.

I thought, "My goodness, what does he want me to do as an Elder?"

So I took him out to breakfast, sat him down, and asked him.

I said, "Why do you want me to become an Elder? What do you want from me?"

He said, "Nothing. I didn't ask you to become an Elder because of what I want you to do. I asked you to become an Elder because of what you're already doing. And who you already are. If you don't know what that is, then I've asked the wrong person."

He was that blunt.

I knew who I was. I knew the calling on my life. It took me a little bit of time to ask God what my next step was.

If there's any description for what an Elder is in the Scriptures, it's this: spiritual oversight.

I see Kingdom Builders as a spiritual issue. Getting this group of people together who are the core of the core to finance and advance the Cause of Christ.

I began to clearly see my role as an Elder within Hillsong Church. I started by looking at all our campuses around the world. I realized we had these great churches doing amazing things, but not one of them had Kingdom

Builders. And, I wondered out loud, "What's wrong with these pastors? Why haven't they got Kingdom Builders?"

The lights went on in that moment.

God revealed to me, the reason these churches didn't have Kingdom Builders is because I hadn't carried the message to them yet. I hadn't launched it. That's when I knew what my calling and mission was as an Elder.

Fast-forward a few months later, and I'm at Hillsong Conference. It's the busiest week of the year for Pastor Brian. Thirty thousand people all wanting a piece of his time. I end up getting 30 minutes with him face-to-face over another coffee.

And, I say to him, "I think I know why our churches don't have Kingdom Builders yet."

He replies, "Why don't they have it yet, Andrew?"

I say, "Because I haven't gone to launch it yet. I think it's my role."

And you know what he said?

"I think you're right. Go for it."

The funny thing is, Pastor Brian told me some years later that he didn't think I could do it. He didn't know how I was going to do it. I didn't either. But I did know I could go tell my story.

And that has been the catalyst.

STOCKHOLM SERENDIPITY

I am speaking at a Kingdom Builders launch at our campus in Stockholm. There's a lady sitting on the front row who starts sobbing when I start talking about Matthew 6:33. She gets up and leaves the room.

After the meeting, the pastor says to me, "I've got a key guy, called Henry, who I'd like for you to take to dinner tonight."

So he introduces me to the guy and it's the bloke who was sitting by the woman who was balling her eyes out.

I'm thinking to myself, "God, are you kidding me?"

I say, "Hi Henry, it's nice to meet you. Who's the blonde-haired woman who was sitting by you during the meeting?"

He says, "That's my wife."

And, I say, "I'll only go to dinner with you if she's coming." I always believe it's vital to speak to both the husband and wife in these situations.

He says, "Okay."

At dinner, Henry says, "For the month leading up to this Kingdom Builders launch, God had told us to fast. And, every single day, for the past 30 days, we have read Matthew 6:33. So when you came out with that verse it just floored us."

He looked me dead in the eyes, "We're in."

Over the years, he has been by far my protégé in Kingdom Builders. He's flown all over the world at his own expense. He's carried my bags. He's sat in hundreds of one-on-ones with couples. He's been a sponge.

Just this year, he traveled with me to Amsterdam and I told him, "Alright, mate. You're speaking tonight. The first 10 minutes you're on."

He and his wife were the first couple outside of Australia to "get it".

SEEING GOD AS YOUR EVERYTHING

Some of you are reading this and probably thinking, "That's great, Andrew. What a lovely story. But, God's not working like that in my life."

Is He not? Are you sure? I want to challenge you that maybe you haven't yet stepped over that line to trust God to be your everything. Maybe He's your "everything" minus one thing, or two things...

Choose Him to be:

Your Source.

Your All.

And, you know why God isn't moving and working like that in your life?

You're still trying to do it on your own. You're still trying to figure it out. You're still fighting and doing it in your own strength.

It'll never work trying to go it on your own.

You see, it takes surrender. Which is a funny thing. Because when someone surrenders, they usually throw both arms up in the air. Just like when you're in worship with both hands raised.

And, when you have both hands raised, you can't hold on to anything. You can't struggle or fight. You can't grasp the things of this world.

You simply have to trust God.

To allow Him to be your Everything.

That's what Kingdom Builders is all about. Remember, it's a heart condition.

Worship, by definition, literally means "of highest value". So, you have to ask yourself, "Is God first in my life? Is He of highest value?"

How you answer that question determines everything in your life. Worship isn't just about singing songs and serving at church on Sundays.

Nope.

It's a total surrender of everything for Everything.

When Susan and I stepped over the line and I finally got out of God's way, our everything changed. If we can do it, so can you.

SERVING AND SPEAKING

I've continued to serve at church. At the Hillsong Conference, my job was to drive the guest speakers around the city and to their hotels. I got nominated to drive this couple from South Africa, Pastors André and Wilma Olivier.

Turns out they have a large multi-campus church in South Africa.

Most of the people who volunteer to drive for the Conference are college students. I was a lot older, of course, and when André and Wilma got in my car, we just clicked.

I drove them for seven or eight years when they came into Sydney for the Conference. And, over the years we've become friends.

One day, I got an email from André's executive assistant inviting me to come to their church and speak at their Gifted Givers weekend. They promised to cover my travel and accommodation expenses.

I was floored. So I rang André up, "Are you serious?"

He says, "Andrew, I know your story. You've got something to share. And, I want my people to hear it."

I'm like, "Oh, okay. I'll come."

I go tell Susan and she says, "I'm coming." So I booked her a ticket and we went.

This was the first time I had ever shared my story as a guest speaker. I was physically ill before the talk because of my nerves. My mouth was so dry. I must have drunk two liters of water while I was speaking those 40 minutes.

But, it really impacted these people. So much so, that André interviewed me on Sunday during all five services.

Not only that, he took Susan and I on a three-day safari to thank us for making the journey over and sharing our story.

God then did something I just couldn't believe. They handed me an honorarium for sharing my story with his congregation.

I was floored.

Are you kidding me, God?

I would have come for nothing. But I think God wanted to affirm I was on the right path. When they handed me the envelope, I asked, "What's this?"

They said, "It's your honorarium."

I didn't expect it and I thought, "This is ridiculous!"

When I saw how impacted people were by me sharing my story, I realized, "Andrew, this is what you're called to do. This is it."

And people weren't just blowing smoke. God was moving in their lives. People, just like Susan and I, were hearing the call to finance the Kingdom.

That's when I knew this is now my next step. God was telling me to continue to give, but to dedicate the next season of life to raising up other givers across the planet.

WHAT ABOUT YOU?

What are you still holding onto?

What are you putting before God?

What is holding you back from going "all-in" with Him?

Whatever that thing is...

Ego.

Your career.

Stuff.

Whatever.

It will never satisfy.

Never.

Because there can only be one, true God in your life.

IT'S NOT ABOUT
THE MONEY

———

The number one issue in the church today is finances.

Within Christendom, the devil has done a great job of creating confusion around finances.

Why?

Because he knows the truth.

He knows if the Church actually grasps what they have ahold of, then his job is finished.

You only have to look at what Hillsong Church has done with one percent of the congregation.

What if Kingdom Builders grew to 10% of Hillsong givers? What if it grew to 20%? Can you imagine how many lives would be changed, churches planted, communities transformed?

Can you imagine?

Money is the linchpin.

Recently, I was speaking at a church in Perth about Kingdom Builders. I was in my last one-on-one meeting with a couple who had come to hear me speak. Just that morning, the wife of the couple I was meeting with had to drag her husband to hear me speak. His mind was blown. So much so, that he's the one who said, "We gotta meet with this guy!"

We sit down and the lights come on. Up to the point of hearing me speak, he had believed the lie that the church just wants your money. The church doesn't want your money.

No.

The church wants you to get your heart right with God. As a consequence of getting your heart right, you'll give. But it's a byproduct of having a changed heart.

Remember: Kingdom Builders is a heart condition!

I know in every single room I get up to speak in, I'm going to encounter someone like this husband in Perth, who has an incorrect mindset about money. And, I know God wants me to dispel the lie that the devil is spreading. I want the Holy Spirit to hit them right between the eyes with truth.

And, the truth is when you realize how blessed you are, you can't help but bless others. You can't help but give.

FROM IN TO "ALL-IN"

I would say 99% of people who are Kingdom Builders are already serving in some part of the church. They're already in.

When I show up and share my story, I'm just helping

move them from "in" to "all-in".

I used to be one of the confused. Sure, I served. Sure, I tithed. But I never saw God as my one and only Source.

God says, "Do you want to put your hand up?"

He asks us, "How big of a conduit do you want to be?"

You see, the tap of blessing is on full. It's us who determine how much of God's blessing is poured out in our lives. And, this type of faith is an "all-in" kind of faith.

The Gospel of Mark tells a story about an encounter Jesus has with a rich young man who comes to him wanting to know the secret to eternal life:

> As he went out into the street, a man came running up, greeted him with great reverence, and asked, "Good Teacher, what must I do to get eternal life?"
>
> Jesus said, "Why are you calling me good? No one is good, only God. You know the commandments: Don't murder, don't commit adultery, don't steal, don't lie, don't cheat, honour your father and mother."
>
> He said, "Teacher, I have—from my youth—kept them all!"
>
> Jesus looked him hard in the eye—and loved him! He said, "There's one thing left: Go sell whatever you own and give it to the poor. All your wealth will then be heavenly wealth. And come follow me."
>
> The man's face clouded over. This was the last thing he expected to hear, and he walked off with a heavy heart. He was holding on tight to a lot of things, and not about to let go.

Looking at his disciples, Jesus said, "Do you have any idea how difficult it is for people who 'have it all' to enter God's kingdom?" The disciples couldn't believe what they were hearing, but Jesus kept on: "You can't imagine how difficult. I'd say it's easier for a camel to go through a needle's eye than for the rich to get into God's kingdom."

That set the disciples back on their heels. "Then who has any chance at all?" they asked.

Jesus was blunt: "No chance at all if you think you can pull it off by yourself. Every chance in the world if you let God do it."

Peter tried another angle: "We left everything and followed you."

Jesus said, "Mark my words, no one who sacrifices house, brothers, sisters, mother, father, children, land—whatever—because of me and the Message will lose out. They'll get it all back, but multiplied many times in homes, brothers, sisters, mothers, children, and land—but also in troubles. And then the bonus of eternal life! This is once again the Great Reversal: Many who are first will end up last, and the last first."

(Mark 10:17-31)

Here's the hard truth: going "all-in" is going to cost you.

However, the promise of God is that whatever you give up will be multiplied many times over.

Susan and I have seen it in our own life.

And, I've seen God do it countless times in the lives of other Kingdom Builders across the planet.

So, don't be like the rich young man who couldn't give up his everything. Trust God, instead, to be your everything and watch what happens.

THE TRUTH ABOUT FINANCES

It was 1996 when Kingdom Builders started. Hillsong Church was 14 years old and had one Australian campus. Yet, Hillsong was globally known, even back then, for our music. Today, we are a global church who has a local impact in New York, Los Angeles, London, Stockholm, Moscow, Barcelona, Buenos Aires, and many other cities all over the planet.

My personal belief is that one of the major reasons for this is Kingdom Builders.

The over and above offering is what Kingdom Builders is about. It literally is what has made the difference when taking Hillsong Church global.

I've learned that if you can't be generous when you have a little, you will never be generous when you have a lot.

I've met people all over the planet who say, "When I get to this level financially, then I'll become a Kingdom Builder."

I can tell you that when they get to that point, they don't give.

Why?

Because it's a much bigger amount.

The truth about finances is it's not limited. But so many people believe they are. So they don't live a generous life.

Maybe that's you.

Maybe you don't know the truth about finances.

Maybe you don't realize that God has the tap on full blast. And, He's looking for people who are already living a generous life. Because He can trust them to continue to give proportionately.

You probably don't have a lot because you cannot be trusted with more.

Another lie the devil wants you to believe is you have to be rich to give.

Kingdom Builders is not about equal giving; it's about equal sacrifice. It's not about the size of the check you're writing; it's about the size of the sacrifice you're making. A single person who is working hard to provide for their family is just as capable as the individual who owns the big business to write a sacrificial check. It's a misconception to see it in currency amounts.

That's the kind of confusion the devil wants to make in your thinking.

An equal sacrifice means a level playing field. The number is irrelevant.

God will test you in the little and allow you to be faithful in the little. He will test you with a little more and allow you to be faithful in the more. Then, He will test you in the much and allow you to be faithful.

THE DEVIL'S PLAN

The devil hates to see you succeed. He will do everything he can to distract, disappoint, and contain you.

His ultimate goal is to kill you.

With Christians, the devil has figured out it's far easier to just contain you. And the easiest way to do it is with your finances.

If you're not stretching...

If you're not making a difference...

If you're not taking ground...

If you're not taking faith steps...

Then the devil doesn't need to disturb you in your safe, little world. In your comfortable little life.

Can I tell you the scariest place for a Christian to be?

The scariest place for a Christian to be is to be comfortable.

And, trust me I know. I can say this with confidence because that was me for 31 years. Until I decided to rip the lid off.

I don't know about you, but I don't want to let the devil contain me. I don't want to live a safe, little life. I don't want to settle.

No.

I want to live a life where God has to show up. I want to receive what He's promised me. I want to live an "all-in" life on the edge of my seat.

The Scriptures teach us that the devil has a plan to steal, kill, and destroy us. But, the good news is that God's plan is to give us an abundant life—a life overflowing with grace and provision (see John 10:10). Which is why you need to consider which plan you're living today.

REVIVAL

The Church around the world right now is seeing revival.

I've seen it with my own eyes.

People are waking up to God's plan for their lives. Serving, giving, and sacrificing to advance the Kingdom.

And, you have an opportunity to be a part of God's plan. To be a Kingdom Builder.

God has taught me that revival is not about meetings. It's not about activity. It's not about getting people excited.

God has shown me that revival is about the heart of an individual. And, the easiest way to know what's in a man's heart is to look at the fruit of his life.

Jesus says three things about those who trust Him—His true disciples:

You'll recognize them because they obey His teaching.

You'll recognize them because they love one another.

And, you'll recognize them because of the fruit in their life.

Revival is about your heart being surrendered, fully committed, totally transformed by the True Source.

What does the fruit of your life say about your faith?

Remember: Kingdom Builders is about the heart. It's

about living a generous life. Being a blessing because you've been blessed. It's not about finances.

It's about giving out of the overflow.

Giving sacrificially.

Giving without strings attached.

When you grab ahold of this concept and truth, you'll put your hand up. You'll become a bigger conduit for God's blessing. And, your life will be radically changed.

People will clearly recognize something has changed in you.

The word revival literally means "to live again".

People will see the obedience, the love, and the fruit in your life. You will be fully alive once again. Fully God's. And your life will be marked with generosity.

PRIORITIES AND PLANNING

———

My priorities changed when God got ahold of my heart.

The biggest regret of my life is that I missed my kids' early years. I was working my tail off in my own strength. Ignoring the fact that I was a husband and father first.

Today, through following God, prayer, and discipline, I don't work on Mondays or Wednesdays. Mondays I spend with Susan. And, Wednesdays we spend with our grandson, Dallas. I don't work those two days. I have chosen to make them for family.

I'm not going to make the same mistake again.

Why?

Because my priorities have shifted.

Everything I do now is on purpose.

And, my purpose is to finance the Kingdom.

In order to do that, and do that well, I have to keep my life in order. I have to keep God first. I have to take care of my family. I have to make choices in line with who I say I am and what I say I believe.

This looks different for each person and family and we are all in different seasons of life with varying circumstances. But we all need to make priorities and plan accordingly.

DENTON'S FOUR D's

Daily. Deliberate. Disciplined. Decisions.

Daily is this: when you know your purpose. When you're on mission, it's 24-7, 365 days a year.

There are no days off.

This is your one life. Now everything you do is who you are.

There is no work/life balance. When you're living on purpose, you are who you are. No matter where you're at, you're living each day fully alive and fully on purpose.

What does deliberate mean to me?

Deliberate means intentional. Deliberate means I'm going to be proactive, not reactive. Deliberate means I'm running my diary and I'm not going to let someone else run my diary. Deliberate means I'm planning my day, my week, my month, my year, and the next five years of my life.

It means I'm not letting things happen to me. But, that I'm striving purposefully with God to create a life that is pleasing and honoring to Him.

I'm talking about every facet of my life. Not just my business. But also my family and friendships. I'm structuring everything around my purpose.

If I don't have a plan, life's just going to happen and it's going to bounce from one disaster to the next.

What I've found over the years is there are a lot of people who are really good at mapping things out, but they get paralysis of analysis. They get stuck on the wrong things.

It's not about the plan. It's the intention of the plan that matters most.

Take my health for example. I hate exercise. But I do it. I've chosen to do cycling. Because it's good for me in so many ways. It's camaraderie and accountability. I'm deliberate when it comes to working out with mates.

Now, if you know anything about cycling, you know you have to map out your course, you have to know your heart rate, and you have to know what to eat so you have enough calories to burn. Once you work all of that out, the discipline starts the night before.

The night before, I have to check my bike to make sure it's safe, that the batteries on my light are charged, my tires are pumped up, I have to get all my bike gear together, and I have to make sure my alarm is set for five o'clock in the morning.

But the real discipline is going to bed early.

The daily, deliberate, and disciplined approach works together so that when my alarm goes off, I can make a decision. A wise decision. To actually get out of bed, get on my bike, and ride.

If I hadn't prepared the night before, then I wouldn't

achieve my personal health goal. If I wake up in the morning, and I have not prepared the night before and my tire is flat, what am I going to do?

I'll just go back to bed. Why?

Because it's too hard.

But when I get up and everything is in place, I can quickly throw my clothes on and I'm out the door—it's easy.

The lesson for you is this: do the necessary work beforehand to live life on purpose without excuses or options to back out.

The Four D's are all about making a wise decision—not a stupid one.

The Bible clearly states that wisdom is the principle thing and wisdom is greater than wealth—so in all your getting, get wisdom.

So far in this book, I have shared some of my wisdom. It's my wisdom because I've practiced it. But, to you reading it, it is only knowledge until you apply it! That's where discipline comes into play. Discipline is the key that turns knowledge into wisdom!

FAMILY HOLIDAYS

I apply the same focus when it comes to planning family holidays. I made a choice 24 years ago, after working tirelessly without a holiday for eight years, to never leave a holiday again without booking another holiday.

I realized way back then that the only memories I really had with my family were on holidays. Monday to Friday were the daily grind. There were a few memories sprinkled in like a few birthdays and an anniversary here and there. But, the holiday times with my family are what's most important to us.

Susan and I, still today, try to take a family holiday away together when we can. We plan it together and we book it together.

Why?

Because we want to live a deliberate life.

The bottom line is this when it comes to these Four D's: you get one chance at life. Don't bump through it.

I used to just bump through it. Now, I live on purpose.

DUE DILIGENCE

Jesus tells a story in Luke's Gospel about counting the cost in following Jesus:

> One day when large groups of people were walking along with him, Jesus turned and told them, "Anyone who comes to me but refuses to let go of father, mother, spouse, children, brothers, sisters—yes, even one's own self!—can't be my disciple. Anyone who won't shoulder his own cross and follow behind me can't be my disciple.
>
> "Is there anyone here who, planning to build a new house, doesn't first sit down and figure the

cost so you'll know if you can complete it? If you only get the foundation laid and then run out of money, you're going to look pretty foolish. Everyone passing by will poke fun at you: 'He started something he couldn't finish.'

"Or can you imagine a king going into battle against another king without first deciding whether it is possible with his ten thousand troops to face the twenty thousand troops of the other? And if he decides he can't, won't he send an emissary and work out a truce?

"Simply put, if you're not willing to take what is dearest to you, whether plans or people, and kiss it good-bye, you can't be my disciple."

(Luke 14:25-33)

You see, a lot of Christians think they're givers. They're not. You may be one of them.

Tithing doesn't make you a giver.

Tithing is just bringing back to God what is God's.

I'll say it again: it's the sacrificial "over and above" gift that makes you a giver.

The heart of what Jesus is going on about is counting the cost. Living with discipline. Living with intention. And, making wise choices. Especially, financially.

This is paramount if you want to be a Kingdom Builder.

My pastor, Brian, talks about giving dangerously, not giving stupidly. We talk about due diligence in business where we're going to be calculated in our decision making.

When I make a business decision, I do my research. I do the homework and try to make an informed decision. Once I have at least 75% of the information, I feel confident to move. Because if you wait until you have 100%, it's too late. You've missed the opportunity. But to counter, you don't make a decision with only 7.5% of the information either; that would be stupid.

Most Christians want to wait until they have 100% of the information to make an informed decision.

I've seen so many well-intentioned Christians over the years make stupid decisions. People who say, "I'm going to give $1,000,000 to the church." But they make $100,000 a year. And, that's just stupid. God doesn't honour stupidity.

God honors faithfulness.

That's why I tell people to pledge the 75% and trust God to show up with the final 25%. Don't make a call believing you can cover 7.5% and expect God to cover the final 92.5%.

That's not faith. It's ignorance.

WE SERVE A TRUSTWORTHY GOD

Over the eight-year span of when we wrote that first $5,000 check to writing a million-dollar check, God showed up time and time again.

Which is why you cannot tell me we don't serve a trustworthy God.

When Susan and I decided to trust God fully, to go "all-in", we had to make some faith-filled decisions.

God has proved to me, for 24 years now, that He is trustworthy. I think we only see such a small part of everything. Time and time again, God has shown up. I don't always know how He's going to come through.

I used to be worried. I used to be anxious. But, now all these years later, I know God will come through. I've had so many circumstances where things looked disastrous and then God turned up. Over, and over, and over again.

And, if God turns up in my life and in Susan's life, I truly believe He will turn up in yours.

But, you have to take faith steps.

You have to go "all-in" with Him.

You can't try to do things in your own strength.

By your own power.

There's a great passage in the Old Testament, which sums up everything I'm trying to say:

> "Don't let the wise brag of their wisdom.
> Don't let heroes brag of their exploits.
> Don't let the rich brag of their riches. If you brag,
> brag of this and this only:
> That you understand and know me. I'm God, and
> I act in loyal love.
> I do what's right and set things right and fair, and
> delight in those who do the same things.
> These are my trademarks." God's Decree.
> **(Jeremiah 9:23-24)**

This is the kind of life God is calling you to if you want to be a Kingdom Builder. A life where your testimony—your only story—is about the fact that you understand and know God.

Not that you're smarter than everyone else.

Not that you're stronger than everybody else.

No.

The only thing that counts is building your life around your relationship with God, and His promises for you.

That's the Kingdom Builder mindset.

Can God be trusted?

You bet, He can! But, it's up to you to take the daily faith steps to walk this out.

All healthy relationships are based on trust. Without trust, nothing works. This is especially true of your relationship with God. If you trust Him, you'll take Him at His word.

Jesus said it this way:

> "Are you tired? Worn out? Burned out on religion? Come to me. Get away with me and you'll recover your life. I'll show you how to take a real rest. Walk with me and work with me—watch how I do it. Learn the unforced rhythms of grace. I won't lay anything heavy or ill-fitting on you. Keep company with me and you'll learn to live freely and lightly."
> **(Matthew 11:28-30)**

What is Jesus saying there?

That God can be trusted.

That He's got you.

That everything you've been working so hard for, He's taken care of.

That He knows what you really need. What you're really searching for. And, the abundant life He promises is only possible by walking with Him.

I don't know about you, but this is the life I want. It's the life I've discovered by going "all-in" as a Kingdom Builder.

ADVANCING BACKWARDS

One of the mandates on Hillsong Church is to champion the local Church. It's a Kingdom thing. Not a Hillsong thing. And, I mean the big 'C' Church. Hence, why I don't belong to any other church.

One thing God has shown me from the very beginning is that I haven't pushed this.

I've never asked to go travel to any church and yet, God has literally taken me around the planet to share our story.

Amazingly, my schedule is always full.

My deal with God is this: I'll go wherever any pastor asks me to go. Anywhere in the world. I simply ask the churches I visit to cover my costs. Occasionally, I get an honorarium, but that's not why I go.

I'm not getting paid to take the message of Kingdom Builders to the world.

I'm doing it because I can do it. Because my business is set up in a flexible manner allowing my schedule to be fluid. I am taking faith steps because of what I know.

I could just go surf and spend the days playing with my grandson. I've had people tell me I've earned as much. But, I know in my heart of hearts that I know too much.

I've seen too much.

I believe that to whom much is given, much is required (see Luke 12:48). And, this school dropout, this Aussie tradie, has been given much. So I have much to give.

Because my purpose is the Kingdom, I have to go do this.

I haven't stopped writing checks.

I haven't stopped serving.

I haven't stopped working in my business.

I've simply gone "all-in" with God to advance His Kingdom.

THE CHURCH I SEE

In 1993, my pastor, Brian Houston, wrote these words:

> The Church that I see is a Church of influence. A Church so large in size that the city and nation cannot ignore it. A Church growing so quickly that buildings struggle to contain the increase.
>
> I see a Church whose heartfelt praise and worship touches Heaven and changes earth; worship which influences the praises of people throughout the earth, exalting Christ with powerful songs of faith and hope.

I see a Church whose altars are constantly filled with repentant sinners responding to Christ's call to salvation.

Yes, the Church that I see is so dependent on the Holy Spirit that nothing will stop it nor stand against it; a Church whose people are unified, praying and full of God's Spirit.

The Church that I see has a message so clear that lives are changed forever and potential is fulfilled through the power of His Word; a message beamed to the peoples of the earth through their television screens.

I see a Church so compassionate that people are drawn from impossible situations into a loving and friendly circle of hope, where answers are found and acceptance is given.

I see a people so Kingdom-minded that they will count whatever the cost and pay whatever the price to see revival sweep this land.

The Church that I see is a Church so committed to raising, training and empowering a leadership generation to reap the end-time harvest that all its ministries are consumed with this goal.

I see a Church whose head is Jesus, whose help is the Holy Spirit and whose focus is the Great Commission.

YES, THE CHURCH THAT I SEE COULD WELL BE OUR CHURCH – HILLSONG CHURCH.

This is what the mission of Kingdom Builders is all about.

To champion the local church, led by local pastors,

changing lives in local communities.

You see, the God we serve is a fan of the "least of these" and the "have nots". He's been a God of the underdog throughout history.

From Moses to David, we see the Kingdom of God advancing backwards in the Old Testament. Choosing this one unlikely nation called Israel as His people. They were enslaved, beaten, divided, and wandering around for generations until God Himself shows up in the straw of a manger.

The long-awaited Savior is born to unwed parents in the most unlikely of places. The King of Kings is the son of a tradie like me. His dad, Joseph, was a carpenter. His mom was a teenager. And, they were on the run from a mad king.

If the Scriptures teach us anything, it's that God does the unimaginable with the most unlikely people.

Hillsong's own story is proof of how God works. Twenty-three years ago, we were just one church with one building in the western suburbs of Sydney. Literally, a little faith community most people couldn't find on a map.

Today, we're in more than 30 countries, 120 locations, with over 300 worship services a weekend, and growing every single year.

And, I truly believe we're just getting started.

ADVANCING THE KINGDOM

In Matthew's Gospel, we get an insider's look at how Jesus describes the Kingdom of God:

"God's kingdom is like a treasure hidden in a field for years and then accidentally found by a trespasser. The finder is ecstatic—what a find!—and proceeds to sell everything he owns to raise money and buy that field.

"Or, God's kingdom is like a jewel merchant on the hunt for excellent pearls. Finding one that is flawless, he immediately sells everything and buys it.

"Or, God's kingdom is like a fishnet cast into the sea, catching all kinds of fish. When it is full, it is hauled onto the beach. The good fish are picked out and put in a tub; those unfit to eat are thrown away. That's how it will be when the curtain comes down on history. The angels will come and cull the bad fish and throw them in the garbage. There will be a lot of desperate complaining, but it won't do any good."

Jesus asked, "Are you starting to get a handle on all this?"

They answered, "Yes."

He said, "Then you see how every student well-trained in God's kingdom is like the owner of a general store who can put his hands on anything you need, old or new, exactly when you need it."

(Matthew 13:44-52)

Yes. The Kingdom of God is worth selling everything for. Like the treasure in the field and the priceless pearl, when your eyes are opened to Kingdom purpose you'll never be the same.

But if you notice, Jesus uses the word *hidden.* I think it's because so few Christians realize Jesus is talking about what's inside of them. I think God sees potential in the hearts of men. I know He saw it in this big, ugly Aussie before I could see it in myself.

And, I believe the Kingdom is hidden in plain sight today. When your eyes are finally opened like mine, well, it changes everything.

Your life will be turned upside down and inside out.

You'll have clarity on what it means to live the "good" life.

You'll also have wisdom to know what you need and how to help others. This is the Kingdom Life. This is the purpose I was searching for 24 years ago.

And, our lives have never been the same.

Sure, it's been difficult.

But it's been worth it every step of the way.

And, I've come to learn that every step is a faith step.

Faith is the spiritual word for trust. And, when you take a small faith step, what you're declaring is that you trust God. That He's your Source.

With every little faith step, you move away from trying to do it in your own strength and you move towards the way of the Kingdom.

So, take a faith step and actively serve in your local

church.

Take a faith step and tithe.

Take a faith step and sacrifice your time and your resources.

Take a faith step and have your pastor's back.

Take a faith step and let go of anything that may be holding you back from grabbing ahold of the life God is calling you to.

Go from "in" to "all-in".

You only have this one life. Why waste it chasing the things of this world? Why waste it trying to build your own little kingdom? Why waste it chasing after the things that don't last?

Wake up.

Turn around.

And, start heading in the opposite direction.

That's what I mean by advancing backwards.

ADVANCEMENT WON'T ALWAYS MAKE SENSE

There's a story in the Old Testament where Israel is about to go to war (see Judges 7). Gideon is the leader at the time and the fighting men under his command number about 32,000. To prove how powerful He is, God commands Gideon to send some of his troops home.

So, Gideon asks 22,000 to head back home.

God still isn't satisfied. He commands Gideon to test

the remaining 10,000. God tells him to bring the men down to the water. The majority of them (9,700) lap up the water with their tongues, but 300 cup the water in their hands to drink.

God tells Gideon to only keep the 300.

Now, one little detail you need to know is that the enemy of Israel was the Midianites. Their army numbered 120,000.

You read that right. Even with Gideon's initial full force of fighting men, he was an underdog at 4:1 odds.

But remember, our God is a God of the underdog. He can do exceedingly more than what we can even imagine.

So, here we see Him increase the odds to 400:1

The math simply doesn't add up. But, that's the amazing thing about God. He doesn't need numbers.

He doesn't need odds in His favor.

No.

He's looking for people prepared to faithfully advance. Even if it seems impossible. Unlikely. And, backwards.

That day, 300 of God's chosen men defeated 120,000 enemies.

Sounds a lot like Kingdom Builders.

God is also looking to do the impossible in your life. He's looking to see if you're going to be a person He can use. If you're ready to sacrifice and take a step of faith.

And, one after that.

And, another one after that.

I've come to realize that most Christians will be like the 31,700 who were sent home. But, the core of the core—

the Kingdom Builders—will sacrificially advance the Kingdom.

I don't know about you, but I want to be someone God can use. I want to take small faith steps every day. I want to see God do the impossible in my life and the lives of my children.

I don't want to run away from opportunities and blessing.

Susan and I want to be people of faith who trust God in good times and in bad. Who advance the Kingdom even if it seems backwards.

And, I know it won't always make sense.

But, that's why it's called faith.

I used to have a neighbor who would always yell out to me when he saw me, "Denton, I want your life."

This guy had no idea of the sacrifice and the heartache, which Susan and I had been through, but I think he could clearly see something different about us. I think he could see the blessing of God in our lives.

I guess he could see the Kingdom hidden in us.

PART TWO

THE PARTNERS

MY SPOUSE

——

My wife, Susan, has been the driving force from day one.

Early on in our marriage, we're a couple years into Kingdom Builders together with a young family and we want to step up our commitment to giving.

Remember, I'm just a plumber. It's all I know how to do. I've got no other qualifications. What else can we do?

So, Susan and I are sitting around the table one night and talking about how we can step up.

And, we follow the logical chain of thought...

The plumber works for the builder. And, the builder works for the developer. So, who makes more money? The developer.

So we say, "Okay. Let's do that."

Susan asks, "Who do we know who is a developer?"

There happened to be a guy at church who would end up buying a big block of land and building a duplex. I mention him and say, "I'll give him a call in the next week and see if I can get a meeting with him."

Susan immediately replies, "Call him now."

I reply, "I can't call him now. I happen to know he's at another church member's house having dinner."

Susan says, "Oh. Well, that's okay. He lives just down the street. Go around there now and ask him."

And, I say, "I can't go around there now. They're having dinner."

Susan shoots back, "Do you want this or don't you?"

I drive around to my neighbor's house where the developer is having dinner and I knock on the door. My neighbor comes to the door and says, "Hi, Andrew. How can I help you?"

I say, "Well, I'm actually here to talk to your guest."

And, my neighbor says, "Does he know you're coming?"

I say, "Nope."

He says, "You know we're having dinner, right?"

And, I say, "Yep. I'll just be one minute."

He stares at me for a moment. "Okay. I'll go get him."

The developer comes to the door and says, "G'day mate. How can I help you?"

I say, "Listen, Susan and I want to step up our giving and we want to get into property development. I know you do a little bit of it and I was wondering if I could have coffee with you this week?"

He thinks for a second and replies, "I looked at a project today. It's too big for me. And, it's too big for two of us. Do you know a third person?"

I reluctantly say, "Yes."

He says, "Cool. Let's have lunch tomorrow and bring that third person. I'm going to go back in and finish dinner now."

I say, "Great, thanks."

I go home and I relay the conversation to Susan, explaining that I need to find a third person.

She says, "Phillip."

I say, "Phillip, who?"

Susan replies, "Phillip, your brother."

And, I come back, "What about Phillip my brother?"

And, she says, "He's your third person."

I say, "He's not going to be interested."

She goes, "Ask him."

Phill is 26 years old at the time. He's already a millionaire. Onto his third house as a builder. Very successful. He's living in a big house, which he built. Everyone thought he was a drug dealer because his house was so big and he was so young.

So, I go around to Phill's house and knock on the door. He comes to the door and says, "Hey bro, how can I help you?"

"Listen, Susan and I want to get into property development so we can step up our giving with Kingdom Builders. I went around and talked to a developer tonight. He has a potential project that he thinks is too big for two people, so he's looking for a third. I went and asked Susan who our third person could be and she suggested you."

Phill looks at me and says, "What? You're kidding? I've just been talking to Melissa today and I said that I couldn't keep up this pace, working these hours, day in, and day out. That I needed to be in a business that has more flexibility that I can operate from anywhere.'"

That conversation was 21 years ago. We've been in business together ever since. Andrew and Susan, and Phill and Melissa.

So, the point of this whole story is this: we just took a step.

A faith step.

And, it was my wife who encouraged me to act. I affectionately call it The Susan Factor.

Throughout the Scriptures, God tells us that it's not good for man to be alone. From Genesis to Proverbs to Paul's writing in the New Testament, God talks about the power of a godly wife.

Over and over in our life together, Susan has prayed, worked, and stood beside me every step of the way.

She taught our kids to fear God and live generous lives.

She encouraged me to risk, grow, and give.

She modeled the way.

Proverbs 31:10-31 talks about the kind of woman God uses to build the Kingdom:

> A good woman is hard to find,
>   and worth far more than diamonds.
> Her husband trusts her without reserve,
>   and never has reason to regret it.
> Never spiteful, she treats him generously
>   all her life long.
> She shops around for the best yarns and cottons,

and enjoys knitting and sewing.
She's like a trading ship that sails to faraway places
    and brings back exotic surprises.
She's up before dawn, preparing breakfast
    for her family and organising her day.
She looks over a field and buys it,
    then, with money she's put aside, plants a garden.
First thing in the morning, she dresses for work,
    rolls up her sleeves, eager to get started.
She senses the worth of her work,
    is in no hurry to call it quits for the day.
She's skilled in the crafts of home and hearth,
    diligent in homemaking.
She's quick to assist anyone in need,
    reaches out to help the poor.
She doesn't worry about her family when it snows;
    their winter clothes are all mended and ready to wear.
She makes her own clothing,
    and dresses in colourful linens and silks.
Her husband is greatly respected
    when he deliberates with the city fathers.
She designs gowns and sells them,
    brings the sweaters she knits to the dress shops.
Her clothes are well-made and elegant,
    and she always faces tomorrow with a smile.
When she speaks she has something worthwhile to say,
    and she always says it kindly.
She keeps an eye on everyone in her household,
    and keeps them all busy and productive.
Her children respect and bless her;
    her husband joins in with words of praise:
"Many women have done wonderful things,
    but you've outclassed them all!"

Charm can mislead and beauty soon fades.
   The woman to be admired and praised
   is the woman who lives in the Fear-of-God.
Give her everything she deserves!
   Festoon her life with praises!

This is Susan. She's been a God-send and my best friend since I was a teenager. I cannot imagine life without her.

When I do my one-on-ones after I give my Kingdom Builders talk, I always ask to meet with couples.

Why?

Because of the "Susan Factor".

I know there are other Andrew and Susan Dentons out there who God has called to finance the Kingdom. And, it's usually the wife who gets it first.

SUSAN'S VISION

Proverbs 29:18 says:

   If people can't see what God is doing,
      they stumble all over themselves;
   But when they attend to what he reveals,
      they are most blessed.

This would sum up my life with Susan.
Period.
Vision is the power of seeing. Literally, it's walking

with God. Hearing from him. And, living in response to His will for my life.

Susan does this.

I do this.

And, the result is we've been blessed to be a blessing.

When I first met Susan, she could see in me what I could not see in myself. I told her verbatim, "As long as I'm on the tools and I don't have to deal with people, I'm happy."

And, she's thinking to herself, "Oh, dear. Well, that's not in my life-plan. But let's see what God can do with this diamond in the rough."

So, she pushed me to say yes to a multi-level marketing business. While we didn't have great success in the business, Susan knew I would walk away with certain business, management, and public speaking skills.

For five years, I was doing my plumbing job during the day, working on my own plumbing business in the afternoon, and hustling in the side-business at night.

It was tough.

But, Susan could see a way forward for us. She could see beyond where we were at the time to where God was calling us to. She realized the only way we were going to get ahead was to stop trying to do it on our own.

Susan was ready for success. And, so was I.

It was about this time where I began to see what God was showing her all along. I stopped the side-hustle, humbled myself, and got on board with what God was calling us to.

That year, Kingdom Builders started.

EQUALLY YOKED

In Genesis, we see it's not good for man to be alone. God gives Adam, Eve.

Well, God gave Andrew, Susan.

And, let me tell you—God knew I needed someone to push me, encourage me, love me, and walk beside me. Someone who wouldn't let me settle. Someone who was as stubborn as I was.

I've learned life doesn't work without an equal.

A partner. A co-laborer.

Over and over in our life together, God has spoken to Susan and me. And, over and over we've been on the same page. Over and over we've given, served, worshipped, and sown together.

The Apostle Paul writes about having an equal partner:

> "Don't become partners with those who reject God. How can you make a partnership out of right and wrong? That's not partnership; that's war. Is light best friends with dark? Does Christ go strolling with the devil? Do trust and mistrust hold hands? Who would think of setting up pagan idols in God's holy Temple? But that is exactly what we are, each of us a temple in whom God lives. God himself put it this way:
> > "I'll live in them, move into them;
> > "I'll be their God and they'll be my people."
> **(2 Corinthians 6:14-16)**

Susan would describe me as loyal, hard-working, and a good friend. I would describe her as generous, godly, and intuitive.

This is as much her story as it is mine. Really, it is the story of us working together to take faith steps. We're on the same team. We have the same vision.

Yes, life has been challenging.

Yes, life hasn't always worked out the way we wanted it to.

Yes, we've been frustrated.

But, we've also trusted God.

And, each other.

MY CHILDREN'S CHILDREN

———

Here are just a few of God's promises over and over in Scripture to look after the children of the faithful:

> God, your God, will cut away the thick calluses on your heart and your children's hearts, freeing you to love God, your God, with your whole heart and soul and live, really live. God, your God, will put all these curses on your enemies who hated you and were out to get you.
>
> **(Deuteronomy 30:6-7)**

> "Can a mother forget the infant at her breast,
>   walk away from the baby she bore?
> But even if mothers forget,
>   I'd never forget you—never."
>
> **(Isaiah 49:15)**

> All your children will be taught by the Lord,
>   and great will be their peace.
>
> **(Isaiah 54:13 NIV)**

But God says, "Stop your incessant weeping,
    hold back your tears.
Collect wages from your grief work." God's Decree.
    "They'll be coming back home!
There's hope for your children." God's Decree.

(Jeremiah 31:16-17)

My son, do not forget my teaching,
    but keep my commands in your heart,
for they will prolong your life many years
    and bring you peace and prosperity.

(Proverbs 3:1-2 NIV)

Point your kids in the right direction—
    when they're old they won't be lost.

(Proverbs 22:6)

I once was young, now I'm a graybeard—
    not once have I seen an abandoned believer,
    or his kids out roaming the streets.
Every day he's out giving and lending,
    his children making him proud.

(Psalm 37:26-27)

Listen, dear friends, to God's truth,
    bend your ears to what I tell you.
I'm chewing on the morsel of a proverb;
    I'll let you in on the sweet old truths,
Stories we heard from our fathers,
    counsel we learned at our mother's knee.
We're not keeping this to ourselves,
    we're passing it along to the next generation—

God's fame and fortune,
    the marvellous things he has done."

(Psalm 78:1-4)

Religious scholars estimate there's close to 3,000 promises from God in the Bible. I don't know about you, but I think this is good news.

It means God can be trusted.

He wants to bless us.

Susan and I have seen it over and over in the lives of our children. We've seen it in the blessing of two godly daughter-in-laws and our son-in-law.

And, we're even getting to see it now in the lives of our grandchildren.

I spend every Wednesday at home with Dallas. I mean every Wednesday he is spending it with Pop. I had no idea what I missed out on when my kids were young. All the hours I put in trying to create a life, I missed out on real life. And, I've committed to not making the same mistake again. I can't even begin to tell you what a blessing grand-children are.

THE DENTONS

If you've spent any time at Hillsong's main campus in Sydney, you'd have for sure run into part of my family. There are heaps of us. My father was a pastor on staff at the church, all of us kids are involved, and now, so are our kids' kids.

Take our three children who came to us through marriage...

Jono married an American, Kmy. She's a God-fearing Texan through and through. She came out for Hillsong Bible College and Jono pursued her like crazy. She'd tell you she said "yes" to Jono because of our family. The moment she walked into our house, she felt like she was at home. And, even though she really liked Jono, Kmy says it was the family who got her over the line to start dating him.

Elisabetta originally entered our family as Anna's friend. She moved away, came back, and then fell in love with our second son, Mitch. She was drawn to how hard-working and faithful our kids were, especially Mitch. And, she's been a very special gift to our entire family ever since they got together.

Then there's Ehsan, Anna's husband. Like how most fathers feel, no man was ever going to be good enough for my baby girl. But, Ehsan is getting close. He's learning. I met this young man through a Kingdom Builders event. He did a bit of work with me at the house. Turned out he had noticed Anna and she had noticed him, but he was too afraid to ask for her number. So, I gave it to him. And, he's not wasted the opportunity.

Ask any of our children or their spouses and they'd tell you the Dentons are known by our commitment to church and how close we are as a family.

We've always tried to instill a united front for our kids.

We loved them through discipline. And, we have made family a priority in everything we do...

Sunday lunches.

Family vacations.

And, we're in one another's lives through thick and thin. The highs and lows. Birthdays, anniversaries, and little celebrations of every sort.

We're not perfect. We don't pretend to be. But we are kind. We are generous. We are forgiving.

And, we are family.

BLESSED TO BE A BLESSING

When our children were just little kids, Susan and I would pray over them and ask God to make them, "The head, not the tail. To be blessed, so they could be a blessing. To be kind and generous" (see Deuteronomy 28:13).

We wanted to teach our kids to work hard, so they could have the resources to help others. To come from a place of abundance, not a place of lacking.

We taught them to take care of what they had so they could eventually take care of others. To be wise with their resources. And, to save.

You see, the greater your capacity, the greater the blessing. A simple lesson, but one we wanted to model in the way we lived.

One of the things we did for them, and still do to this day, is have an open-door policy in our house. Their friends are always welcome in our home.

We want to make room for those in need.

We want our home to be a refuge.

We want to live a generous life.

We want to be able to host people.

We want to bless others.

And, our kids have learned to do the same thing.

God makes a promise to Abraham. He basically says, "I'm going to rewrite history through your children's children" (see Genesis 12).

God is going to bless generation upon generation of Abraham's children.

Why?

Because of Who God is. It's in His nature. It's what He does.

And, because of Abraham's faith.

I think most Christians out there live small lives. Never risking or believing for a bigger life. Never hoping or praying for generations upon generations of their descendants to know and trust God.

I used to have such little faith. Faith is about capacity. It's about how much you can be trusted. How much you can be blessed.

Susan and I discovered that God tests us.

He will give you a little and see how you'll use it.

Then He'll give you a little more.

And, then a little more.

Before you know it, He'll be blessing you beyond anything you can ask think or imagine. He's done it over and over in our life and in the lives of our children.

Why?

Because we were faithful.

Because we trusted His promises.

Because we are "all-in" with Him.

Because we're living on purpose.

I believe God is looking for men and women who will take a small step of faith.

Who will refuse to chase after quick fixes and instant gratification.

Who will give up trying to "make it".

And, instead trust the One who made everything.

God wants to bless you.

He really does.

IT'S NEVER TOO LATE

Jesus tells a story in the Gospels about a wealthy farmer who had two sons (see Luke 15:11-22). One son was dutiful, obedient, always available, and around to help his father. The other son was a bit of a wild card. A rebel.

The younger son comes to his father and asks for his inheritance. The father doesn't argue. He gives him what he asks for and the son goes on his merry way. Jesus tells us that the younger son lives it up. He wastes what he's been given on prostitutes, drinking, and wild living.

Until he reaches the end of the road with nowhere to turn but home.

So he heads back to his father, who sees him coming. The father does something astonishing; he welcomes the son home with open arms and throws the prodigal son a party.

Well, the older brother gets wind of what's happening and throws a tantrum. He refuses to go in, so the father goes out to him as well and assures him of his place and of his grace.

Like most of Jesus' parables, there's layer upon layer of meaning to be found in this famous story.

God is a generous Father who is ready to bless you.

God doesn't play favorites and is ready to forgive you no matter how much of your life you've wasted.

And, God cares about your heart. The older son had a jealous heart. The younger son had a rebellious heart. God is looking for open hearts.

Remember: Kingdom Builders is a heart condition.

It's about surrender, humility, teachability, and trust.

I'm a dad with three sons and three daughters. Fortunately, none of my kids or their spouses have rebelled against me or God.

But, let me tell you, I would love them the same. And, trust they'd come back just like the prodigal.

So, if you're reading this and you think you're too far gone for God to use, well, you are mistaken.

God is in the restoration business. He'll turn your life around and upside down. But, He's waiting for you to wake up. To stop selling yourself short. For you to quit wasting the blessing.

You don't have to carry a generational curse into the future. You can break it.

All it takes is a small faith step.

All you have to do is come to your senses like the prodigal and head back home.

Your Heavenly Father is waiting. Watching. And, ready to come running so He can bless you.

And, make you a blessing.

Just ask my kids.

MY PASTOR

——

My pastor is not perfect.

Actually, he's not even close. For starters, he's a Kiwi. But I don't hold that against him. I married a Kiwi, so I'm actually quite fond of New Zealanders.

One thing he is, for sure, is a visionary.

The Scriptures tell us in Proverbs 29 that without vision, the people perish (see v.18). Which tells me the opposite holds true.

Way back in the early nineties, God gave him a picture of the future. A vision.

Specifically, a local church with a global reach. A Kingdom-minded movement for the Cause of Christ. A network of churches across the planet who were in major cities of influence impacting millions for the Gospel.

What started out as a handful of Christians meeting in a school auditorium in the northwest suburbs of Sydney has now grown to more than 150,000 people worshipping together across every continent. One house, many rooms.

Hillsong Church is a global family.

But, my pastor is local. I know him by name. He knows me. And, I trust him.

Why?

Because as I've already said, I can see the fruit of his life and ministry.

Kingdom Builders is an extension of Pastors Brian's and Bobbie's heart for the nations. To see significant, apostolic churches in local communities that cannot be ignored because of the significant contributions they are making.

One of the biggest reasons why Hillsong has gone global is a handful of Kingdom Builders caught my pastor's vision. And, we were able to come from a position of strength to make that vision a reality.

Most pastors lack Pastor Brian's vision.

I truly believe Pastor Brian is a once-in-a-lifetime leader. It's his heart and God's calling that has raised up a group of Kingdom Builders. I have been riding his coattails for over 24 years.

I trust him.

And, I've got his back.

Pastor Brian has never asked me or any Kingdom Builders to do anything that he himself is not prepared to do. He's been a Kingdom Builder himself from day dot.

And, I know, there have been times in the life of Kingdom Builders where he has been the largest giver in the group.

He is a generous soul. There have been countless times

where I have had to fight him over the bill for dinner. And, it's his money, not the church that's paying.

One of Pastor Brian's personal mantras is: "Spending is seasonal. Generosity is a lifestyle." He and Bobbie live this out.

THE UNOFFENDABLES

Pastor Brian supports Kingdom Builders fully. But, he doesn't treat us any differently. He makes time for us. He honors us.

We have an annual retreat as Kingdom Builders. It's the only time Pastor Brian ever announces anything about us as a group. He spends the entire weekend with us. And, we satellite in to the rest of the campuses on Sunday.

He usually shares a bit about us, but it's not a big to-do, just a simple shout out that we're a small group who believe our purpose is to finance the Kingdom.

Which creates a bit of curiosity amongst the rest of the church.

You see, we're the core of the core.

We're the group who has stepped over the line and gone from "in" to "all-in".

I like to call us the "Unoffendables".

No matter what goes down, we have Pastor Brian's back.

This doesn't mean I always like what Pastor Brian says.

Pastor Brian preached a sermon one Sunday entitled,

As for Me and My House, We Serve the Lord. I'm there taking notes with my Bible open. And, he says to the entire congregation, "You want to see an example of As for Me and My House, We Serve the Lord?" He turns and points to where Susan and I are sitting, and continues, "Andrew and Susan Denton over there. Just watch them." He walks off the platform.

Then he has the audacity to send me a text, "I gave you a bit of a wrap this morning."

I text back, "A wrap? You just dumped me in it, man. I can't give anyone the bird in the carpark anymore. Everyone is gonna be watching me now."

That was Pastor Brian though. He already had the insight—that I was one of the "Unoffendables".

But, it also hit me. Everyone was already watching me. They were wanting to see if I was for real.

Susan and I are.

And come hell or high-water, we've got Pastor Brian's back.

KINGS AND PRIESTS

Pastor Brian loves to help people. Loves to see them live up to their potential. Ultimately, he's committed to do everything he can to reach people and connect them with Jesus.

He believes for miracles.

He leads from the front.

He travels, speaks, and writes all for the Cause of Christ.

His role is broad and global today. But, his mission hasn't changed over the 37 years he's been the pastor of Hillsong. It is the mission of Kingdom Builders.

From the Ukraine to Spain to North America to Australia, he's championing the Cause of Christ. He's building the Kingdom.

His role is the vision. He's a priest. My role as a Kingdom Builder is provision. To finance the Kingdom.

Pastor Brian calls it "Kings and Priests".

The role of the priest throughout Scripture was to connect people with God. That's Pastor Brian's heart. That is his calling. His ministry.

My role as a Kingdom Builder is to help finance the Kingdom. To raise the above and beyond offering so the message of the Gospel can be taken across the globe.

The two work together. Vision and provision. A picture of the future and the means to make that picture reality.

Maybe, just maybe, that's your calling, too?

To provide. To work hard. To sacrificially give so that your pastor's vision can become a reality.

And that's the role of a king—to protect and provide.

THE ROLE OF THE PASTOR

I made a decision 16 years ago to employ people smarter than me.

I learned that from Pastor Brian. He has always had these super talented pastors and leaders working with him.

People would ask him, "Aren't you threatened by them?" And, Pastor Brian would say, "No. It's an honor to have such intelligent and creative people to work with. Because of their gifts, Hillsong Church is able to innovate, progress, and flourish. Honestly, they make me look good. I do lead from the front, but could not have the kind of reach and insight without my colleagues."

That kind of leadership takes confidence.

It takes humility.

And, it takes an incredible capacity to identify and attract the right kind of talent. To nurture that talent. And, to get out of the way.

I believe the reason a lot of pastors fail is they are too ego-driven. They have too much pride. They have to be in control.

That's not the kind of leader God promises in Jeremiah, chapter 3.

I've also seen Pastor Brian be a strong and decisive leader. People don't want to follow a wishy-washy leader. They want to follow a leader whose vision is straight and true.

Pastors need to be persistent in seeing gold in people. I've seen Pastor Brian do this over and over again throughout the years I've been following his leadership. And, it works.

Why?

Because it raises up the next generation of Kings and Priests in the Church.

Pastors also need to listen to collective wisdom. This requires the courage to ask for help. They must have an attitude that it's not all about them. They don't know it all. They don't have all the answers.

I remember four or five years ago, I said something out of line. And, Pastor Brian addressed me about it.

He said, "You've got a big mouth on you, Denton."

I said, "Yeah, you're right. I'm going to apologize."

He looked at me and said, "Andrew, you know what I love about you the most? You are teachable."

Pastors also need to be able to dig deep and know when to fight for the future. Fiercely unstoppable. Relentless.

Pastors must also be able to prioritize their own well-being. This is about discipline. And, being strong enough to say "No." Which comes down to being able to make the gutsy decisions.

Pastors need to be leading from the front. Just like Pastor Brian, in that they won't ask anyone else to do what they're not willing to do themselves.

To do more than they're paid to do. To give more than they have to. To try harder than they want to. To consume less than they desire to. To help more than they need to. And to waste less time than they ought to.

Finally, I absolutely believe pastors must be intuitive. They have to be able to see into things. This requires a deep and rich prayer life.

If you're a pastor reading this, know that the people

you're trying to lead will never go further than you do. Your flock will never out pace you. Never out give you. Never out serve you.

If this list creates a sense of desperation in you, then that's a great thing.

God is a God of transformation. He promises to give us a new heart and a new spirit. And, that promise applies to you.

What I love about Pastor Brian and Bobbie is they live this out.

Their vision for Hillsong Church goes beyond them.

It has to.

And, it's not about them. It's about the Kingdom of God advancing. The Cause of Christ going forward. And, the people of God living out the Gospel in places of significance and influence all around the globe.

GOD'S PROMISE OF VISION

Luke captures a prophetic word from Joel about the Church:

> "In the Last Days," God says,
> "I will pour out my Spirit
> on every kind of people:
> Your sons will prophesy,
> also your daughters;
> Your young men will see visions,
> your old men dream dreams.

When the time comes,
I'll pour out my Spirit
On those who serve me, men and women both,
  and they'll prophesy.
I'll set wonders in the sky above
  and signs on the earth below,
Blood and fire and billowing smoke,
  the sun turning black and the moon blood-red,
Before the Day of the Lord arrives,
  the Day tremendous and marvelous;
And whoever calls out for help
  to me, God, will be saved."

(Acts 2:17-21)

If your church is not growing, I'd ask you to check your heart.

Are you believing the promises of God?

Are you taking faith steps?

How big is your vision?

Do you actually have a vision?

Is your vision too small?

My friend Lee Domingue has a saying: "The Pastor sets the Vision, but the Kingdom Builders set the Pace."

Vision is your ability to see the future. To clearly articulate what you see back to your church. And then call, equip, and empower them.

Don't miss this point.

Most churches get stuck at 300 people because most pastors are too afraid to dream bigger than what they have the capacity to lead. If this is you, you're actually hamstringing your congregation by your inability to grow yourself.

If you don't want to grow personally in your own spiritual walk and your own capacity, then you're holding back your congregation. I'd say you're ripping them off. Robbing them of what God wants to do in their lives and in the life of your community.

Hillsong's reach is beyond anything we could ask, think or imagine because Pastor Brian hasn't stopped dreaming. He hasn't stopped believing. He hasn't stopped increasing his own capacity.

Over the years, I've seen Pastor Brian grow his capacity. And, as a result, we have a global reach. A global family.

One house, many rooms.

MY NETWORK

———

Dieter Conrad and I first met seven years ago after a Kingdom Builders talk I gave at his church.

Dieter had all these massive dreams. And, I remember thinking, "Whoa. Really?"

He was "all-in". He had the right heart condition.

But, he hadn't done anything significant yet. At the time, he was still working for someone else.

I didn't meet up with him again for several years. When I met up with him four years later, he was the largest giver at Hillsong Church Germany. He sat on the board for Compassion Germany. He sat on the board of Vision Rescue for Germany.

And, in that time since I last saw him, he had started his own business and was earning seven times what he was earning before. Not double. Seven times.

His life had completely and utterly been turned around when he found his purpose to be a Kingdom Builder.

He's an amazing man. A great story.

I met another young man in Germany who drove three hours just to have a 15-minute meeting with me. We had met two years previously and I remember asking him, "What are you believing God for? How big are your dreams?"

And, he replied that he would like to work for a specific company.

Two years later when we met up, he said, "Andrew, my prayers were answered. I'm going to be working for that company. But, that's not all. I'm going to be their CEO. Talk about above and beyond what you can ask, think or imagine."

He said, "Two years ago, what was above and beyond what I could ask, think or imagine was to even work for that company. But to go there and start as the CEO... It's just ridiculous."

Then there's Juan Marcos in Barcelona. He was a single guy when I first met him. In a business. Never thinking he could write a €2,000 check.

Today, he's married to a beautiful Russian young lady. And, he's writing €20,000 and €30,000 checks. His business has gone to just another level as a Kingdom Builder. He knows his purpose.

These are just three stories from hundreds I could tell you. Which is why I won't ever stop doing what I'm doing—telling my story and the story of Kingdom Builders.

I love that people are waking up. Their lives are changing. They are beginning to grasp their purpose. Watching God rip the lid off their lives. Seeing God do abundantly more than what they could ever ask, think or imagine.

I love seeing people trusting God. Taking faith steps.

And, I love seeing pastors who are hungry. Desperate for Kingdom Builders.

PARTNERSHIP IN THE GOSPEL

Today, I feel the weightiness of this message. I know the impact to the churches I'm speaking at. But, I also know that I'm speaking to specific people. Men and women just like you. Who are searching for something more. Something meaningful. Something worth dedicating your life, your career, and your family to.

I also know that the devil is not happy with me speaking it. I know that I am a marked man. He doesn't want people to hear this message. Which is why I pray every time I get up to speak.

I ask God to open hearts and minds to hear the truth and power of this message.

I know that if just one person, that one percent of the congregation, grasps this message the difference it can make is huge. But, what if half the room gets it?

That's what I'm praying for. Those are the partners I'm looking to find.

I was in Konstanz, Germany, just a little tourist town similar to Queenstown, New Zealand, where my wife is from, sharing the message of Kingdom Builders.

At the time, it felt obvious that the financially influential and more established city of Dusseldorf would be a wiser choice of headquarters because there was an intensity of wealth and a far greater population.

However, it was in Konstanz where I felt led by God to prophesy over the congregation. I prayed, "Just as Baulkham Hills, a small suburb outside of Sydney, has led the way when it comes to Kingdom Builders, I believe that out of little Konstanz here, you will not just finance Germany, but surrounding countries, too."

Now, a prophecy should only ever confirm what's on someone's heart.

The Lead Pastors, Friemut and Joanna Haverkamp, were there and little known to me at the time, it had been impressed on their hearts also that they were not to move to Dusseldorf, but to stay in Konstanz. That decision had felt unconfirmed until this time. My message confirmed what was already on their heart.

This message of Kingdom Builders is a message of obedience. Hearing the voice of God, and living in response.

I'm living it by taking the message around the globe.

And, I've seen partners in the Gospel, Kingdom Builders, all over the planet, step up and go "all-in".

TESTING GOD

As I travel around sharing this message of financing the Kingdom, I often get asked, by either a husband or a wife, "How can I be on the same page with my spouse when it comes to giving?"

I always turn to the book of Malachi:

> Bring the whole tithe into the storehouse, that there may be food in my house. Test me in this," says the LORD Almighty, 'and see if I will not throw open the floodgates of heaven and pour out so much blessing that there will not be room enough to store it.
>
> **(Malachi 3:10 NIV)**

I ask the couples, "Have you tested God?"

He says to test Him.

And, I share the same story. I'm sitting in church on a Sunday and I look across the auditorium where I see a young man who has been in church for awhile. He's been in Bible College and he's about to head back to Europe to start a church.

Well, God just puts it on my heart to sow into his ministry. And, I'm like, "Cool, God. How much?"

He tells me the figure. Boom. Just like that.

Then I say, "Alright, God. You know the deal. Tell Susan. She's got to know."

I'm expecting to get an elbow immediately in church. Nothing happens. Service ends and I'm still waiting for something to happen.

We head outside to the parking lot together.

Nothing.

We get in the car and I'm about to start the ignition when Susan says, "Hey, I believe that God is telling me today we should sow into Stuart's ministry."

And, I'm like, "Oh, really? How much?"

Then Susan replies with bang on the dollar of the amount God had revealed to me. I cried, because I'm a big softy.

We were obedient and we did it.

He comes around on a Sunday and has family dinner. On the way out, I hand him a card with the money inside. He has no idea what's in the card.

It had a huge impact on Stuart.

So much so, that his grandparents wrote us letters months later thanking us for what it meant in his life and ministry.

Now, I've told that story everywhere I've traveled for quite some time. That's the story I tell whenever people ask me how they can be on the same page and unified.

Firstly, as a husband, I had my spiritual antenna on high to hear from God. And, I heard from Him.

Secondly, I tested God. "Alrighty, God. Then you tell Susan."

Thirdly, she had her spiritual antenna on high and she heard from God, too.

Fourthly, we were obedient—we actually did it.

As a result, a man and his ministry were blessed.

A few years back, I was in Europe speaking. Stuart found out and rung me up. He asked if he could come hear me speak and I said, "Of course." Then I thought to myself, "I need to come up with a new story."

So I prayed, "God, help me figure out what I need to

share."

God shot straight back, "Why? What's wrong with that story?"

"Well, Stuart's going to be there tonight, God. That will be a bit weird, won't it?"

God was like, "Do you trust me or don't you?"

So I give my talk and of course, the question about couples being on the same page comes up as I'm standing right in front of Stuart. I tell his story. Halfway through it, he's thinking to himself, "He's talking about me. He's talking about me."

When it came time in the part of the story about his grandparents writing me, he never knew they had done it.

So, after the meeting, he grabs me and says to me, "Andrew, you don't know what that did for me. The money you and Susan gave to me was the exact amount I needed to get my life sorted and my ministry started."

It came from being obedient and in unity. On the same page spiritually. Equal partners in the Gospel.

MY PROTÉGÉ

I've traveled all over the world now sharing my story, supporting the local Church, and championing this calling of financing the Kingdom. And, the remarkable thing I've found in every church I stand up to speak at is the handful of people just like Susan and I who have been waiting to hear this simple message.

Time and time again, I've seen future Kingdom Build-ers self-select. Put their hands up. And, say, "I'm in."

One of those guys, who I've already mentioned here in the book, is Henry Brandt. He's the believer from Stockholm who took me out to dinner with his wife. They had been fasting and praying for the Kingdom Builder's launch, and God had given them Matthew 6:33 as a pas-sage to meditate on and pray about.

When I stood up to share, it unlocked something in their heart. God was confirming in them, through me, that the Kingdom Builder's call was for them.

Henry has since traveled with me all over America, and Europe. He's carried my bags, listened to me speak, and sat with me through hundreds of one-on-ones.

What I love about Henry is that he is teachable. I can-not even count how many times he's heard my story, but I see him there taking note after note on his phone.

I genuinely believe God has called other Henry Brandts out there. Men and women who are putting God first in every area of their lives. Who have stepped over the line. Who are walking closely with God every day.

Henry calls me one of his best friends in life. I call him a brother in Christ who gets it.

He's an example to his church in Stockholm. And, be-cause he gets it, they get it. Which is one of the reasons why Kingdom Builders in Stockholm is growing faster than anywhere else in the world.

I also call Henry my protégé. But the truth is, God is raising up, and calling out men and women all over the planet to champion the Cause of Christ in the local Church.

I genuinely believe there are Henrys everywhere.

Today, I have men and women all over the world who are begging to be challenged to not just be Kingdom Builders in regular giving, but to also, like myself, be raising up the next generation of Kingdom Builders across the globe.

AN OPEN LETTER TO PASTORS EVERYWHERE

———

Dear Pastor,

Your church is waiting for you to do the soul-searching, life-giving, earth-shaking work you've been called to.

They are eager to get behind your God-sized vision to advance the Kingdom beyond what even you can ask for, think or imagine.

A handful are desperately anticipating and praying for the opportunity to be stretched, challenged, mobilized, and called out to give, go, pray, and lead.

Yes. Their eyes are glued on you. They are watching to see if you are who you say you are. And, that you'll do what God has called you to do. They want to know if you are for real. They want to see what you'll do first. If you will...

Serve first.

Give first.

Dream first.

Pray first.

Go first.

And, they truly believe and want to go "all-in". They really do.

But, they're waiting.

Yes. They're waiting to be challenged by a God-sized vision that calls out the best in who they are and what they believe is possible. They are waiting to be called to life out on the edge. Kingdom life.

The life they've read about in the Scriptures.

The life you preach about week in and week out.

The abundant life God promises over and over in the Scriptures.

But they need you to paint a picture of where God is calling your church to.

What your vision for them as a community of sold-out, "all-in" believers really looks like. The big-hairy-audacious-vision that scares you.

You know. The one you surrendered your life and calling to be a part of. That God-sized vision that is beyond your wildest dreams and aspirations. The one that requires God to show up and show off. The vision that you've been too afraid to speak out loud.

Your playing small doesn't do anyone any good. Especially your church family. Your inability to dream big is causing them to play small, too. They are tiptoeing around the truth, because you are.

Don't let your ego get in the way.

Don't let your lack of faith paralyze you.

Don't let anything big or small stop you.

Do whatever it is that you need to do to hear from God. To dream with Him. To see the potential that He sees. To capture the hearts of the people He's entrusted to your care.

Don't shrink back.

Don't play small.

Don't waste another Sunday. Another sermon. Another moment.

Get on your knees. Open up your heart. And, ask for the impossible.

Then take what God speaks to you back to your people. Speak that vision into reality. Call out the best in them. And, invite them to join you in making that God-sized dream a reality.

Your people are waiting.

God is waiting.

And, deep down you're waiting.

Now is the time.

Stop procrastinating and start believing.

You have been called to so much more. To build the Kingdom. And, to raise up Kingdom Builders.

Sincerely,

Andrew & Susan Denton

PART THREE

THE PRACTICE

FAITH IS SPELLED R I S K

———

Over the years, I've learned that faith really is spelled RISK. And, by risk, I mean taking wise risks. Ones that make sense. Not foolish ones.

The Hebrew word for wisdom literally means, "to live life skillfully".

So when you risk, you shouldn't be dumb about it. You should use your head. Follow God's heart. And, take steps of faith. But steps that make sense. Faith steps at the edge of your comfort zone. Faith steps not just with your finances, but with every area of your life.

The writer of Hebrews tells us this about risk and taking steps of faith:

> It's impossible to please God apart from faith. And why? Because anyone who wants to approach God must believe both that He exists and that He cares enough to respond to those who seek Him.
>
> **(Hebrews 11:6)**

Fear and faith are the same emotion. And, how you approach God says a lot about what you believe about Him.

Do you really believe that He cares about you?

Do you really trust that He has your best interests in mind?

Do you really know that He will respond?

Do you really think all of His promises are meant for you?

If so, then you'll be willing to take faith steps.

What I've worked out is you cannot be faithful if you're fearful. I believe you cannot have a little bit of fear and be faithful. That little bit means you're fearful.

The same is true about having a little bit of faith. You cannot have that little bit of faith and be fearful. They simply don't coexist.

You have to make the decision.

And, it's not easy. But you have to choose.

You can be fearful when life and the devil throw things at you, but you have to have a faithful attitude.

Every time I meet with couples after a Kingdom Builders event, I ask them the same question at the end of our conversation, "Will I see you again?"

This tells me a lot about whether they are being fearful or faithful.

Believe me, I've been there.

Early on I could speak "Christianese" with the best of them. But my faith always had two or three back-up plans from Andrew.

I really came to the understanding that true faith was

truly trusting in God. If God didn't show up, then I would be in trouble.

For me, my first faith step was quitting my third business. I was going to work a third less and spend time with my family. I believed God and that He would bless that decision. And, He did.

I'm not sure what your first faith step is, but I know you have to take it.

REAL RISK

The real risk is to go through life and play it safe.

I try to live this out every day. I know too much now to play it safe. I've experienced God turning up. Over, and over, and over again. I know how faithful He really is. I also know too much to just surf each day and play with my grandkids. I know too much to be that selfish.

Which is why Susan and I are still risking today.

We're still serving. We're still living a generous life. We're still writing checks. And, I'm still going all over the planet sharing this message of financing the Kingdom.

I cannot play it safe.

I don't freak out about anything any more.

I'm still taking faith steps. Susan and I are right out there on the edge. We're not afraid, we're not anxious, we're not fearful.

I know what I'm meant to do. I'm getting all of my priorities covered. I'm a "touch it once" person. I've learned to be effective.

If you're going to really risk, then you have to be efficient.

I've been an early riser most of my life. I've had to get deliberate in doing things. I totally crush my day before I've had breakfast.

Why?

So I can be free to advance the Kingdom. To travel the world with this message.

I believe God is calling you to take real risks, too. And, if you're deeply honest you want to risk. You want to take faith steps. You want the abundant life God promises us in the Scriptures.

When I became a Kingdom Builder, I stopped playing it small and safe. I stopped working, thinking, and living from a scarcity mindset. I started taking wise risks.

When I look back on my faith journey and the risks I've taken, I can clearly see that God was waiting on me.

When I decided to stop my career as a plumber, I completely got out of the self-sufficiency game. As much as I had enjoyed my time as a tradie, I knew I needed to take a faith step toward a different career—one that God was calling me to.

Over a six-year period, God blessed me for burning my boats. Not giving myself a way back. Going totally in with Him.

Today, I have a Godly confidence.

He hasn't always turned up when I've wanted Him to, but He's always been right on time.

You know, I still make plenty of stupid mistakes, but

I'm risking in the right way. I'm taking faith steps believing that God will show up.

The older I get, the more I realize how little I really know, but my Godly confidence is such that I don't worry. I just believe.

START SMALL

Matthew tells a story about one of Jesus' miracles in his Gospel:

> When they came to the crowd, a man approached Jesus and knelt before him. "Lord, have mercy on my son," he said. "He has seizures and is suffering greatly. He often falls into the fire or into the water. I brought him to your disciples, but they could not heal him."
> "You unbelieving and perverse generation," Jesus replied, "how long shall I stay with you? How long shall I put up with you? Bring the boy here to me." Jesus rebuked the demon, and it came out of the boy, and he was healed at that moment.
> Then the disciples came to Jesus in private and asked, "Why couldn't we drive it out?"
> He replied, "Because you have so little faith. Truly I tell you, if you have faith as small as a mustard seed, you can say to this mountain, 'Move from here to there,' and it will move. Nothing will be impossible for you."
> **(Matthew 17:14-20 NIV)**

The real miracle is faith. Did you see what Jesus said about faith?

If you have even just a little bit you can do the impossible.

People come to me all the time and ask me, "How do I write a $1,000,000 check?"

And, you know what I tell them? "Write the $5,000 one first."

Over the years, I've met too many people who believe that when they get that next promotion or get their business to turn over a certain amount, then they'll become a Kingdom Builder. And when they get to that point, they still don't do it, because they're making more money.

People I meet often say, "Well, I can't afford to tithe."

I say simply, "I believe you cannot afford not to tithe. If you can't be trusted with a little, then you'll never be trusted with a lot."

If you're not tithing when you're making $100 a day, then how will you be able to when you're making $1,000 a day? It comes back to fear and faith. And whether you truly trust God or not.

If you can't be generous when you have a little, then you'll never be generous when you have a lot. It's too hard then. Just too hard.

You have to have the maturity. You have to grow personally. And, you have to start now with what you have.

I'm not sure what the impossible is in your life. I don't know what demons you're facing. But, I do trust what Jesus said in the passage above. If you have just a little bit of faith, you can do anything.

I don't know what your faith step is, but God does. The best advice I can give you is to use what's in your hand. Just take a faith step.

A man rang me up once and said, "Andrew, can I have a coffee with you?"

I said, "Sure." He was a builder and I figured we'd have a lot in common.

We met and 10 minutes into the conversation, he's asking me all of these basic questions about building. So I said, "Bro, as a builder you should know all of this stuff."

He said, "I'm not a trained builder. I have an IT background."

So, I asked him, "Then what are you doing with a building company?"

He said, "Well, I saw all these builders who were making good money so I bought a building company."

I said, "Mate, I see all these guys in IT but I didn't buy an IT company. I like steak but I didn't buy a butcher's shop. Bro, what are you doing?"

He went broke. The grass looked greener over there. And, he thought, I'm going to do that. He made a foolish choice. And, took a bad risk.

God's given each of us gifts. So, don't try to do what other people are doing. Do what you know. Keep taking faith steps.

Use what's in your hand.

You've got to work with what you've got.

Romans 8:28 (NIV) states:

And we know that in all things God works for the good of those who love Him, who have been called according to His purpose.

You have to ask yourself, are you on purpose? Are you doing what you're called to do? You've got to love what you have to do.

I'm in construction. I love building things. I love seeing an idea come out of the ground and become a real, tangible thing. It's what I do.

I don't design what we build, because I'm not creative. But if you give me a plan, I can build anything.

What are you gifted at?

What small steps do you need to take?

How are you trusting God with what you have right now?

These are all important questions. Faith questions. Life questions.

Remember, there's no such thing as a "wrong step".

Most people are waiting for the perfect timing. You've probably even said to yourself, "It's just not the right time."

You know what I've found? There's no such thing as the "right time" or the "wrong time". Just take the step anyway.

I've waited at times and it was a stupid decision. You see, if God's behind it, He's going to make it work. He can accelerate things when they need to be accelerated. And, He can slow things down when they need to be slowed down.

He's God.

He's in control.

He's got you.

And, He's waiting for you to take that small faith step and trust Him with the gifts and resources He's entrusted you with.

What are you waiting for?

UNDER ATTACK, RIGHT ON TRACK

The number one thing you can be sure of is when you take a faith step you're going to come under attack. And, this is a good thing, because you'll know you're right on track.

The devil doesn't want you to advance the Kingdom.

The devil doesn't want you to go "all-in" with God.

The devil doesn't want you risking.

The devil wants you to be comfortable, content, and complacent.

So when you step out in faith, you're putting a target right on your back. Susan and I have experienced this first hand. We've experienced attack personally, physically, and relationally.

If you think you're above getting taken out by the devil, that's the time you're about to get taken out.

In a matter of about 18 months, I was in four different accidents. The last one almost killed me. Broken ribs, broken fingers, broken wrists, and a torn hamstring later, I know that the devil is out to get me.

At that point, I remember thinking to myself, "What's next? What's next?"

I knew I was right on track. And, that the devil was trying to kill me.

You need to understand explicitly that the devil hates when you're faithful and will actively work to make you doubt your faith, doubt your calling to finance the Kingdom, and doubt the very promises of God.

The Scriptures tell us that the devil actively seeks to "steal, kill, and destroy you" (See John 10:10).

When you put your hand up to serve, you can guarantee that heartache and hardship are coming your way.

But, you can also rest assured that God is true to His promises.

1 Peter 5:8-11 (NIV) talks about the attack and what God will do:

> Be alert and of sober mind. Your enemy the devil prowls around like a roaring lion looking for someone to devour. Resist him, standing firm in the faith, because you know that the family of believers throughout the world is undergoing the same kind of sufferings.
>
> And the God of all grace, who called you to his eternal glory in Christ, after you have suffered a little while, will himself restore you and make you strong, firm and steadfast. To him be the power for ever and ever. Amen.

Ephesians 6:11–17 (NIV) instructs us on how to combat the devil when we're under attack:

> Put on the full armor of God, so that you can take your stand against the devil's schemes. For our struggle is not against flesh and blood, but against the rulers, against the authorities, against the powers of this dark world and against the spiritual forces of evil in the heavenly realms. Therefore put on the full armor of God, so that when the day of evil comes, you may be able to stand your ground, and after you have done everything, to stand. Stand firm then, with the belt of truth buckled around your waist, with the breastplate of righteousness in place, and with your feet fitted with the readiness that comes from the gospel of peace. In addition to all this, take up the shield of faith, with which you can extinguish all the flaming arrows of the evil one. Take the helmet of salvation and the sword of the Spirit, which is the word of God.

Truth. Righteousness. The Gospel of Peace. Faith. And, the Holy Spirit.

These are are our weapons.

What is truth? Truth is a Person. His name is Jesus. And, truth is the Scriptures, the very words of God.

What is righteousness? Righteousness is right living. It's walking with God and being a person of integrity.

What is the Gospel of Peace? The Gospel is the good news of the Kingdom. It's the promise that God is making you whole and holy.

What is faith? Faith is spelled RISK. It's walking with

God no matter what and trusting that He is faithful to His promises.

And, lastly, the Holy Spirit is alive in anyone who is a child of God. The Holy Spirit is there to teach you, guide you, and protect you from the devil.

I'll leave you with Jesus' own words:

> Jesus answered them, "Do you finally believe? In fact, you're about to make a run for it—saving your own skins and abandoning me. But I'm not abandoned. The Father is with me. I've told you all this so that trusting me, you will be unshakable and assured, deeply at peace. In this godless world you will continue to experience difficulties. But take heart! I've conquered the world."
>
> **(John 16:31-33)**

How good is that? Difficulties are promised, but we can rest assured that Jesus has conquered the world.

BUILDING IN
UNCERTAIN SEASONS

———

Mother's Day looks different this year. At the time of writing, the state government of New South Wales in Australia has put in place restrictions in response to the COVID-19 pandemic.

Things can change dramatically in such a short time frame.

From living life as per "normal", to now only being allowed to have two people visiting my home, in addition to my immediate family. Social distancing and hand sanitizers are now a must.

Cafés and restaurants are closed. The way we shop for groceries has changed. I now have to get a quarantine pass in order to take domestic flights between states in Australia. If my construction company wasn't considered an essential service, I wouldn't be able to fly at all.

Church services are different now also. We can no longer gather physically, so are making sure that our online experiences are the best they can be to minister to our congregations and beyond.

Life is now via Zoom, phone calls, and FaceTime.

In February 2020, I was visiting the Hillsong Church locations in Denmark. Several weeks later, I was in Norway and the whole nation shut down the day after I flew out!

The world is feeling the severe impact of restrictions and the ripple effects are far reaching. It's not just my little bubble in Sydney or your little bubble wherever you are on the globe.

This specific crisis has changed the whole world at once!

Embracing a lack of control requires high trust. If we get all anxious, worried, and concerned (all just other names for fear), then the devil has already started defeating us.

Don't be fearful, be faithful!

So much fear is being thrown at the whole world right now. The fear of what "might" happen is causing people to make rash and unwise decisions. We need to build upon God's certain promises, not the world's uncertain predictions.

God knew about this pandemic before we knew about this pandemic. He already has the answers. The best strategies.

It is possible to still remain "all in" when circumstances tell you to get "all out".

GOD ALWAYS TURNS UP

We all want miracles, but don't want to be in desperate situations that need one. But imagine God using even a COVID-19 pandemic to fix other issues in your personal life, business, and finances.

That's what happens when God turns up in a crisis; He provides answers that are even better than we can imagine.

Here's the exciting thing: I am already hearing so many miracle stories during this season from Kingdom Builders who are actually going to be able to give more than their current pledge or more than they have ever given before.

A friend from my church connect group recently shared how the last 18 months have been the worst 18 months in 20 years of business. You can imagine how the pandemic lockdown was making him feel.

However, his business has now just had his best April month ever. In fact, April 2020 has been better than his whole past 12 months.

> Jesus said, "Mark my words, no one who sacrifices house, brothers, sisters, mother, father, children, land—whatever—because of me and the Message will lose out. They'll get it all back, but multiplied many times in homes, brothers, sisters, mothers, children, and land—but also in troubles. And then the bonus of eternal life! This is once again the Great Reversal: Many who are first will end up last, and the last first."
>
> **(Mark 10:29-31)**

Are you feeling like you are sacrificing a lot right now? Troubles will come, but it's not the end of your story. The question is, are you putting yourself first or God first?

During uncertain seasons, we must remember that it's not all about the money; it's about the condition of the heart. Our capacity (what we can give) to be generous may change in crisis, yet our conviction (values and absolutes) regarding generosity remains the same.

There's a businessman I know very well. His name is Sam. In what seemed like a moment, 10 weeks' worth of work was put on hold indefinitely as a result of the COVID-19 pandemic.

Sam shared how he clearly sensed God giving him guidance: "Sam, you're going to give your way out of this." He acted upon this word during the weeks ahead. Sam decided to provide free services for clients while still paying his workers who were at home and unable to work.

I'll never forget calling Sam during this time. I needed some work done on my garage and wanted to give him the job.

"Yeah, I'll come and do it. But only if I can do it for free."

"What? I didn't ask you to do it for free, Sam. I am able to pay you and I want to pay you."

"Oh, I know you can pay me, Andrew. But that's not the point. I want to sow it."

I was astounded. Here's a man who had nothing else in the pipeline. But he was still sowing seeds of generosity in an uncertain season, believing that God would grow a future harvest.

The world of the generous gets larger and larger;
the world of the stingy gets smaller and smaller.
(Proverbs 11:24)

Well, Sam experienced the promise of this verse. On his way home from my place, he got an unexpected call. An offer to complete a significant amount of work that was to start within two days, requiring him to employ 15 people to complete it!

God always turns up in crisis. Sam had to sow seeds first. Then his generosity turned into a harvest of miraculous opportunity and provision.

A DIFFERENT ECONOMY

"That's 25% more than the asking price!"

Leading up to the pandemic restrictions in my part of the world, I had a block of land that I couldn't even give away if I'd wanted to! As Aussies sometimes say, "It was burning a hole in my pocket."

I was losing money on this property, but had no solutions in sight.

Situations like this could make me fearful, but I honestly sleep fine at night. I know God's got it under control. It's not arrogance; it's the Godly confidence that I wrote about previously.

Things that society says should stress you out shouldn't

stress you out because we live under a different economy.

Back to the block of land: at the time of writing, I now have two potential buyers trying to out-bid each other for it. That's right. During an uncertain global season. And as a result, I will potentially walk away with a quarter more than the original asking price.

I'm not sharing this to boast, but to show you how God is able to use all things for good in your own circumstances. And when the provision comes, it comes. There will be no doubt that God has been involved.

Having a Godly confidence paves the way for miracles to take place. I have an expectation that challenges will come, but an absolute expectation that God will take care of it as I make wise choices and declare His promises.

We have unfair advantage; we can pray for God's favor and favor with people. Even the most unexpected of people.

> A good person leaves an inheritance for their
>   children's children,
> but a sinner's wealth is stored up for the
>   righteous.
> **(Proverbs 13:22 NIV)**

The world may say it's all doom and gloom, but we will see unprecedented blessing in the midst of, and as a result of, unprecedented crisis.

We will eventually look back and realize that we were positioned perfectly.

TIME'S A TEACHER AND CRISIS IS A REVEALER

My gray whiskers show two things: I have been living life for a while now and I'm still around to write about it.

Time has taught me that I really can't do this myself. I need God. It's a great place to arrive to. Such a better way to live.

Susan and I were recently reflecting on another crisis that we had to navigate over a decade ago. The financial crisis of 2007-2008. It hit us hard. I remember a year later, literally getting down on my knees and crying out to God to help us.

And He did help us, but not in the way we expected. No money falling down from the sky (that would have been awesome). Instead, He used this crisis to prepare us for future crises.

I've never learned anything in the good times. In the good times, we are all geniuses. But in the tough times, when it costs you personally, that's when you learn the lessons.

We were able to recognize weaknesses in our business model and implemented changes that have now helped and protected us during this current COVID-19 crisis. In fact, we are growing stronger and moving forward during these current times.

Was it easy back in 2008? No! Did it all change overnight? Of course not. But God is faithful. What is "right now" revealing to you? What will you allow time to teach you?

Learning to give, and continuing to give, in tough seasons prepares you to be better able to handle future prosperity and blessing.

There is a cause and effect for everything we do. When we choose to trust, obey, and take those faith steps, vision can still turn into reality, even in a crisis.

This may be hard to read: your character, motivations, and processes are revealed in crisis.

Crisis reveals what you were already putting in place before the crisis. If you were unwise before a crisis, there may be limited ability or capacity to ride out the tough times.

However, if you have been operating your business and finances in a way that is spiritually sound before a crisis hits, you will be in a better position to handle what lies ahead.

It all comes back to the Four D's I mentioned earlier. It's all about living a disciplined life.

> The road to life is a disciplined life;
> ignore correction and you're lost for good.
> **(Proverbs 10:17)**

Here's three absolutes in my own life regardless of the season:

Firstly, I read my Bible daily. Don't underestimate the power of reading your Bible! Read it with an absolute expectation that God is going to speak to you each day.

I refuse to put it down until He speaks to me and gives

me my daily word. I'm living my life in such a way where I'm taking faith steps and the devil is attacking; I need God to speak to me every single day.

My soul needs nourishment just as much as my body needs its daily meals! Yes, we also need resources like other books, courses, podcasts, and sermons, but the Bible must be our foundation.

Once I get that verse, I share it. To my family first through our WhatsApp chat and then to others. I've been doing this for some time now that it's been fondly called Denton's Daily Verse.

Secondly, I pray with Susan daily. I love praying with my wife. So many people are married, but living life alone. The devil wants to separate marriages because he understands the power of that spiritual covenant.

If you're not married, pray daily with two other people who have permission to speak into your life.

Be accountable and transparent. Share from your heart. Have the open conversation first, followed by prayer. It's through honest communication that the Holy Spirit begins to reveal the core issues that shape how we then pray for each other.

We will always have challenges as Kingdom Builders. The devil hates our life of faith. Prayer puts a hedge of protection around you.

Finally, I reflect on my dreams and goals daily. And I can only do this because I have them written down!

And then GOD answered: "Write this.
 Write what you see.
 Write it out in big block letters
  so that it can be read on the run."
(Habakkuk 2:2)

You've got to have goals in all areas of life: ministry, business, family, marriage, health, and finances. You've got to have a clear vision and have dreams to hold on to in crisis. They will stop you from shifting into survival mode.

Without written goals, you won't do the things that you need to do to have a healthy and fruitful life.

Time has taught us and crisis has revealed to us the following: being a Kingdom Builder is not just about building external things for God. It's also about allowing Him to build internal things within our own souls.

Our health is vital. Our physical health, mental health, emotional health, and spiritual health. What do you need to do to become healthier?

Dear friend, I pray that you may enjoy good health
and that all may go well with you, even as your soul
is getting along well.
(3 John 1:2 NIV)

I may have no hair on my head, but I've chosen to remain youthful in spirit! It's a choice.

LET JESUS LEAD AND EMBRACE THIS GOD-LIFE

"Andrew, do you have any advice for Kingdom Builders who are in a bit of a 'mess' right now?" A vulnerable and candid question asked by a young woman not so long ago.

This is the passage of Scripture I used to encourage her:

> Calling the crowd to join his disciples, he said, "Anyone who intends to come with me has to let me lead. You're not in the driver's seat; I am. Don't run from suffering; embrace it. Follow me and I'll show you how. Self-help is no help at all. Self-sacrifice is the way, my way, to saving yourself, your true self. What good would it do to get everything you want and lose you, the real you? What could you ever trade your soul for?"
>
> **(Mark 8:34-37)**

Jesus invites us to let Him lead. This requires humility and obedience.

Seek wisdom, ask for help, start your daily disciplines! Swallow your pride and repent; turn around again. It's never too late to get back on track.

I love that we serve a God of grace. There will be the hard work needed to fix the consequences, but you can still get back on track.

There have been times in my own life where I've had to put my hand up, admit my mistakes, and ask the Lord to lead my life. And then I've needed to obey; whether I see the results of my obedience on this side of eternity or not.

We don't repent and obey just to get blessings; we repent and obey to have an intimate relationship and connection with Jesus.

Let me encourage you with my Aussie slang: get back to God "real quick". There is always hope in a crisis. We can still fruitfully emerge from tough times even if we have made unwise choices.

Get your life sorted. We all know what to do, we just don't do it! The important thing is to realize it; identify it, repent from it, learn the lesson, and keep moving forward with Jesus in the lead.

This is the whole point of the salvation process: we can't do any of this in our own strength. We always need our Savior, Jesus Christ.

> Jesus was matter-of-fact: "Embrace this God-life. Really embrace it, and nothing will be too much for you. This mountain, for instance: Just say, 'Go jump in the lake'—no shuffling or shilly-shallying—and it's as good as done. That's why I urge you to pray for absolutely everything, ranging from small to large. Include everything as you embrace this God-life, and you'll get God's everything. And when you assume the posture of prayer, remember that it's not all asking. If you have anything against someone, forgive—only then will your heavenly Father be inclined to also wipe your slate clean of sins."
>
> **(Mark 11:22-25)**

"Embrace this God-life." If you get your life right, take that next faith step, and trust in Him, He'll take care of you. You'll then be able to build in every season, even in the uncertain ones.

EXCITING DAYS ARE AHEAD

This COVID-19 crisis, and any other crisis, can make Kingdom Builders more strategic, intentional, and effective. I don't know about you, but I'm now using technology to do things that we could have done before, but it wasn't a necessity. Currently, it's now the only option.

Facilities and buildings are not the defining parameters for our churches. This uncertain season has revealed that we now have the capacity, through technology, for a larger audience for the Gospel message and discipleship.

The ability for us to help a whole lot more people has opened up to us. People are more receptive to the Gospel.

This is the time to be sowing! We may not be meeting in buildings, but there is a financial need attached to innovative ways emerging from a crisis.

When our purpose is Kingdom-focused and our spiritual ears and eyes are in tune with the Holy Spirit, opportunities will come to be a blessing.

We aren't just called to give when things are safe. We are also called to build in uncertain seasons.

This is an opportunity for Kingdom Builders to be generous—not to draw back!

IT'S TIME TO BUILD

So you've read this far and I guess you're looking for what you can do next?

Well, my whole goal of writing this book was to carry the message of what it looks like to finance the Kingdom.

My prayer is this little book makes it around the globe to churches everywhere, big and small.

If you're a layperson, like me, you should go straight to your pastor and let him know that you're "all-in". That you've got his back. And, that you're going to commit to giving above and beyond your normal tithes and offerings.

If you're a pastor reading this, you should do an open invite to everyone in the church to share the vision that God has laid on your heart. Don't discriminate. And, ask God to raise up a lead Kingdom Builder who is willing to share their story.

To both of you, I say, "The tap is on full. God is waiting for you to believe. For you to take the first faith step."

Pastor, you're the priest called to give a vision. And, layperson, you're the king called to give provision.

Working together, you can advance the Kingdom in your little corner of the world.

You can raise up an army of Kingdom Builders committed to going "all-in" with God.

You can lead the way by being servant leaders. By taking a step of faith.

And, I believe that first faith step is to gather anyone and everyone you can from your congregation and share this simple message.

I guarantee you'll be surprised by who shows up.

It probably won't be who you think. And, this is a good thing. Because our God is a God who surprises us by using the little and the least of these to advance His Kingdom. Remember: Susan and I weren't millionaires when we wrote our first check. So, don't count anyone out.

Not the tradie.

Not the single parent.

Not anyone.

Just take the first faith step of gathering people together and sharing the vision and your commitment to raise up men and women to build the Kingdom.

I'd encourage you to meet with any individuals or couples after you hold your Kingdom Builders Launch event. Find out what resonated the most with them and then challenge them to take their first faith step.

I typically ask the first question in my one-one-ones. And, I've included a few example questions at the end of the book to help you sort this out.

The real Kingdom Builders will self-identify. They'll put their hand up. They will seek you out. So, be ready for them.

Your job is to just gather people. Then to stand up and share the vision and your simple story of giving.

God will do the rest.

You can test Him in this and see if He's not true to His promises. If He doesn't open up the flood gates of heaven and pour out so much blessing that there will not be room enough to store it.

I've seen Him do it on every continent over the past 24 years of my own Kingdom Builder's journey.

So, I have no reason to doubt He won't stay true to His promises.

The real question is, will you take that first faith step?

Because God is waiting on you.

KINGDOM BUILDERS CHECKLIST

☐ Does the pastor have a vision?

☐ Have you identified one Kingdom Builder to share their testimony?

☐ Have you set a date for the launch?

☐ Have you adequately marketed the event to anyone interested?

☐ Have you set aside 30-minute time slots for one -on-ones to meet personally with those who attended?

☐ Have you created Kingdom Builder pledge cards for people to write out their pledges?

☐ Have you set aside a special weekend to honor and invest in your Kingdom Builders?

☐ Have you shared this book with at least 10 people (the core of the core) from your congregation, and asked them to pray for the event?

☐ Have you personally committed to give above and beyond your normal tithes and offerings?

ONE-ON-ONE SAMPLE QUESTIONS

1. What resonated with you the most from the Kingdom Builders event?

2. Are you on the same page spiritually with your spouse/fiancé? (If married/engaged)

3. What is holding you back from going "all-in" with God?

4. Are you living a fearful or faithful life? Why?

5. What are you believing God for as a result of this simple invitation?

6. Do you pray daily with your spouse?

7. If you're single, do you have two other Godly people to pray with daily?

8. Do you have written goals and dreams for your life?

9. Do you read your Bible DAILY?

ACKNOWLEDGMENTS

My Lord and Savior, Jesus Christ—the ultimate Builder of His Church and my life. Thank you, Pastors Brian and Bobbie Houston, for your leadership that has empowered and released me to discover and fulfill my purpose. Huge thanks to Steve Knox for helping me put my life's message into written words. Celina Mina—thank you very much for turning this book into a reality. Thank you, Karalee Fielding, for your feedback and direction. Tim Whincop—your guidance in the nuances has been invaluable—thanks, mate. I am very grateful, Nathan Eshman, for your audio skills when producing the audio version of this book. Tony Irving—thank you for offering your photographic magic that got my face on the cover. Thank you, Mike Murphy, for pushing me to write the Kingdom Builders journey and message in the first place. Last, but never least—my family and many friends that have encouraged me along this journey. I am very thankful.

ABOUT THE AUTHOR

———

Andrew Denton is a successful business owner and long-time elder at Hillsong Church who has circled the globe sharing a simple message: inspiring pastors and their congregations to live life on a different level and finance the Kingdom. He's also raised three wonderful, God-fearing children alongside his beautiful bride, Susan. As a kid he wanted to be a professional surfer and travel the world; God answered one of those prayers. When Andrew's not cycling, texting Denton's Daily Verse out to leaders around the planet, or drinking a long-black, you can find him enjoying time with his grandkids at home in Sydney, Australia. Relational, honest and straight-forward, Andrew's approach to ministry and life is nothing short of inspirational. His talks have impacted thousands of believers world-wide. Which is why the truths found within these pages will challenge you to become a Kingdom Builder and change the way you serve God forever.

CPSIA information can be obtained
at www.ICGtesting.com
Printed in the USA
BVHW040255130221
600047BV00002B/2